Past and Present

Past and Present

The Challenges of Modernity, from the Pre-Victorians to the Postmodernists

GERTRUDE HIMMELFARB

ENCOUNTER CLASSICS

ENCOUNTER BOOKS

NEW YORK · LONDON

First American edition published in 2017 by Encounter Books, an activity of Encounter for Culture and Education, Inc., a nonprofit, tax exempt corporation. Encounter Books website address: www.encounterbooks.com

Manufactured in the United States and printed on acid-free paper. The paper used in this publication meets the minimum requirements of ANSI/NISO z39.48–1992 (R 1997) (*Permanence of Paper*).

FIRST AMERICAN EDITION

LIBRARY OF CONGRESS CATALOGING-IN-PUBLICATION DATA

Names: Himmelfarb, Gertrude, author.
Title: Past and present : the challenges of modernity, from the pre-Victorians to the postmodernists / by Gertrude Himmelfarb.
Description: New York : Encounter Books, 2017. |
Includes bibliographical references and index.
Identifiers: LCCN 2016040459 (print) | LCCN 2017000061 (ebook) | ISBN 9781594039256 (hardback) | ISBN 9781594039263 (Ebook)
Subjects: LCSH: History—Philosophy. | Knowledge, Theory of. | Truth—Philosophy. | BISAC: POLITICAL SCENCE / Essays.
Classification: LCC D16.8.H6237 2017 (print) | LCC D16.8 (ebook) |
DDC 901—dc23
LC record available at https://lccn.loc.gov/2016040459

CONTENTS

Introduction

A WISE HISTORIAN and a good friend, the late J. H. Hexter, recalling the impassioned political views of some of his colleagues, told me that he did not share their concerns only because he did not have the time or mind for them. Apart from family and friends, he explained, he spent most of his waking hours teaching, reading, and writing about Tudor and Stuart England. He knew more about the relations of the royalty and nobility than about Congress and the president, was more familiar with the Elizabethan Poor Laws than with the American system of social security, was more involved in the debate over the rise and decline of the gentry than the rise and decline of the proletariat. Immersed in the past, he did not have to be cautioned against the "Whig fallacy": interpreting the past in terms of the present, imposing the values of an enlightened, progressive present upon a benighted, retrograde past. Had he ever been tempted to write about the present, he might have been inclined to reverse that order, imposing the values and perhaps virtues of the past upon the present.

That, indeed, is my temptation. More mindful of the present than my friend, I am sufficiently stimulated by the past to relate it to the present. Most of these essays were written a decade or two ago, but the earliest of them, dating back more than half a century, sets the theme for the others. The quarrel between "ancients and moderns," memorialized by Leo Strauss, can be applied to history as well as philosophy. Just as a philosopher today may look to the classics for the enduring truths of humanity, so a historian may find that his past, the period in which he is professionally engrossed, resonates in his own present, the period in which he happens to live. In the same spirit, William James's "once-born / twice-born" adage may be given a larger latitude. Normally confined to the realm of religion, it may be extended to history – to the historian who finds in his study of the past something like a rebirth, a new perspective on the present.

In one way or another, to one degree or another, the essays have the same effect, setting past and present in an active, sometimes adversary relationship to each other. The American "War on Terror" provoked by the 9/11 attack recalls Edmund Burke's war against the "Reign of Terror" launched by the French Revolution. The contrast between those wars, the one pursued resolutely by Burke and the other irresolutely by America, may be seen as an object lesson in history, pitting past against present – in this instance, to the credit of the past.

So, too, Matthew Arnold's defense of high culture, "the best which has been thought and said," as opposed to the "anarchy" of liberalism that recognizes no principle except "doing as one likes," may be read today as a critique of the even more anarchic, unprincipled culture of our own day. Walter Bagehot's analysis of the "efficient" English constitution unified by a single "sovereign authority," unlike the American Constitution where authority is divided by the separation of powers, may be challenging to the new constitution makers, who have to decide between the English and American models. T. H. Huxley's tract on "evolution and ethics" – in effect, "evolution *versus* ethics" – is more pertinent than ever, as the advocates of "scientism" make even larger claims for evolution in particular and science in general.

The final section, "Of This Time, Of That Place" (the title courtesy of Lionel Trilling) reminds us of some of the other tensions besetting modernity. The "democratic disorders" of our time are notably different from those experienced by the Founding Fathers and are even more resistant to the "democratic remedies" envisaged by them. If the hard facts and statistics compiled only two decades ago – about family dissolution and welfare dependency, crime and violence, drug addiction and pornography – have to be updated, it is only for the worse. And if the relations between civil society and the state seemed problematic then, subverting our traditional ideas about the "love of country," they are more so today.

The last (and most recent) essay suggests how far we have come, from a postmodernism that has transformed academia, "deconstructing" and "problematizing" one discipline after another, to a transgenderism that deconstructs and problematizes humanity itself – our physical and social as well as spiritual and moral nature. Having denied the factuality ("facticity," as is now said pejoratively) of objectivity and truth, the post-postmodernist denies reality in all its dimensions. As the events of the past are only "social constructs" "invented" by the historian, or the poem only a "text" essentially created by the reader or literary critic, so the present exists only problematically and purposelessly, without substance or reality, to be created or recreated at will.

In this state of cultural and social "anarchy" (Arnold's word is more apt today than it was then), we may be inspired by the "visionaries and provocateurs" revisited here. The final word may rest with Lionel Trilling, one of the most eminent of our latter-day mentors. Trilling recalls us to the principle that may still liberate and restore us – the idea of truth. "In the face of the certainty that the effort of objectivity will fall short of what it aims at, those who undertake to make the effort do so out of something like a sense of intellectual honor and out of the faith that in the practical life, which includes the moral life, some good must follow from even the relative success of the endeavor."

2016

The Past and the Present

CHAPTER ONE

Leo Strauss:
Ancients and Moderns

—————————■ ▮▮▮▮ ■—————————

IT WAS THE MARK of his age, John Stuart Mill once wrote, that "men may not reason better concerning the great questions in which human nature is interested, but they reason more." Mill was innocent of the faint note of irony that some readers might find in this remark. He intended it simply as an expression of hope and optimism. In the democratic faith of his circle, quantity was held to be as much a good as quality; or at least a prelude to quality. It was all to the good if men reasoned more, particularly if more men reasoned more. Mill and his friends were heartened to watch the flow of newspapers, journals, pamphlets, and books from the presses and into the hands of a steadily growing public. And they decided that what technology had done to promote the habit of reading, science might do to promote the habit of reasoning.

Thus, at a time when political democracy was still in its infancy, ingenious men were already devising schemes for the establishment of a democracy of intellect. The common denominator of this democracy was to be the scientific habit of mind. Knowledge, it was hoped, would be emancipated from the individual knower. Instead of the vagaries of thought by which the privileged few stumbled upon intuitions of truth, there was to be a prescribed logic of inquiry by which all rational and conscientious men could collectively arrive at this truth. The operations of the mind were to become as simple, unambiguous, and anonymous as the operations of the ballot. Having come this far in revolutionizing knowledge, men more enthusiastic than Mill were claiming for their new science not only the superiority of quantity but also the superiority of quality. The boldest of all, Auguste Comte, divided the history of humanity into three stages, of which the first two, the theological and the metaphysical, were sunk in myth, legend, and superstition, and only the third, the "positive age," could aspire to "positive knowledge."

For a century or so we have been living under the new dispensation. Earnest men have favored us with manifestoes and programs for the dissemination of scientific methods, and scores of monographs have labored to apply these methods to the study of man as a political and social animal. There is an even greater abundance of reason abroad than Mill would have thought possible. But in the opinion of some, it is of far poorer quality than Mill could have suspected.

Distressed by the excessive quantity and the too often inferior quality of modern political and moral thought, some malcontents have taken refuge in the past, seeking to liberate men from the new dogma that only through science or democracy, or a combination of the two, can men arrive at the truth. No anonymous or collective enterprises, they insist, can compensate for the genius of old, for the wisdom, inspiration, and insight of individuals. Much of what passes for modern enlightenment, they claim, is superstition and much of what passes for ancient superstition is wisdom. A new "Battle of the Books" is under way, between the "moderns" dedicated to science and the "ancients" to classical philosophy.

In political theory especially, the lines between ancients and moderns, between political philosophers and social scientists, have been sharply drawn. The arch-proponent of the ancients today is Leo Strauss, author of *On Tyranny: An Interpretation of Xenophon's Hiero* (1948) and *The Political Philosophy of Hobbes* (1936), as well as essays on Spinoza, Rousseau, Maimonides, and other thinkers, ancient and modern. One of the many gifted émigrés from Germany, he is a distinguished professor at the University of Chicago, noted for bringing to political philosophy a respect not only for the classics, but also, perhaps more important, for a mode of exegesis and textual analysis that can do justice to them as well as to the moderns.

Political philosophy today is too often written by men who look down upon the past from the superior vantage of the present. Tolerantly (and sometimes not so tolerantly) they explain, so as to explain away, the philosophy of a thinker by reference to the political quarrels of his time or his personal views and dispositions. This is not Strauss's way. On the assumption that great minds – in this lies their greatness – transcend these ephemera, Strauss attends to nothing but their ideas. Great minds are great for all time, not only for their own time. And the basic categories of political thought are similarly eternal and immutable. Natural right or social justice does not change its character just because men's opinions about it have changed. Truth does not change; only beliefs do. "Philosophizing," Strauss invokes Plato, "means to ascend from the cave to the light of the sun, that is, to the truth."

Moreover, we can only hope to understand the truth as the philosopher understood it. If Xenophon, like other philosophers of antiquity, was much preoccupied with the question, "Is the tyrant happy?" Strauss assumes that the question is significant even if it sounds puerile to the modern ear. He finds, in that modest, homely question overtones of the perennial questions of philosophy: the nature of man and his happiness, of pleasure and virtue, morality and nature, justice and power, private and public morality, the natural and the best state, piety and law, the ruler and the ruled. In that spirit, he pursues the common-sense inquiries of Xenophon: If the tyrant must fear assassination, how can he be happy? If he is unhappy, why does he not retire from public office? If he needs power only in order to be secure, how can he be said to be secure when he is in danger of death? If he seeks only sensual gratification, could he not better achieve this in private life? To address these questions, it turns out, is to go to the very heart of political philosophy.

It is no simple task to understand the philosopher as he meant to be understood, for one of the obligations of the philosophical enterprise, Strauss finds, is the occasional veiling, often at critical points, of the real meaning or significance of an idea. There is a body of private, esoteric teachings in most great philosophers that is available only to the prudent disciple and that is concealed from the irresponsible public. When Xenophon seems to be arguing for tyranny, that may be only a device by which to establish the case for law and legitimacy. When Maimonides takes pains to argue for the scrupulous observance of ritual and law, it is perhaps an intimation that ritual and law must be observed even when they cannot be believed. The assumption is that nothing in the text is said or left unsaid heedlessly. Strauss himself, in the style of great philosophy, writes deliberately and precisely, so deliberately that one must read him as carefully as he would have us read others. So deliberately, indeed, that one might almost suspect him of harboring esoteric theories of his own. "I have not dotted all the i's," he hints in his interpretation of Xenophon.

One of Strauss's main services to political philosophy has

been pedagogic. He has taught students to take the great thinkers of the past seriously. And he has taught them that exegesis,
which is the greatest compliment one philosopher can pay
another, can be more productive of insights than the speculations of those who feel that the fact of their having come late
into this world gives them an advantage over those who pre-
ceded them. "It goes without saying," Strauss writes, "that I
never believed that my mind was moving in a larger 'circle of
ideas' than Xenophon's mind." That it can move so freely
within that circle of ideas is praise enough for any man. The
commentator, in the Talmudic tradition, is the philosopher par
excellence, and so it is with Strauss.

A more conventional exegesis is that of a colleague of Strauss's
at the University of Chicago, David Grene, author of *Man in
His Pride: A Study of the Political Philosophy of Thucydides
and Plato* (1949). Grene's is more a historical than a textual
analysis. Both Thucydides and Plato, in his account, are decid-
edly men of their time. In the case of Thucydides, this is no
more than natural. The Peloponnesian War was not only the
substance of his life; it was also the subject matter of his
thought. The case of Plato is different, for it was not his experience in Sicily that made him regard a king as a philosopher,
but rather his philosophy that imposed itself on that experience. It is just this superiority of philosophy to history that is
what is commonly implied by Platonism.

If Grene's method is historical, however, his motive is
always philosophical. The historian, Thucydides, must qualify
as a philosopher to capture Grene's interest. The theme of his
book is that Thucydides at the one end and Plato at the other

7

represent the limits of the movement of political philosophy in the West. At opposite reaches of the mind, they have sought answers to the fundamental questions of political philosophy: What is the natural, or best, political order? How can political power be justified?

The standard interpretation of Plato has the philosopher starting as a mystic and visionary and ending up as a practical man of politics. Grene takes issue with this interpretation. In his view, Plato became not less but more mystical in his later years, more intent upon the ideal – which was the real – world of form and order concealed behind the world of the senses, and more convinced than ever that politics without philosophy was mean-ingless, just as power without justice was intolerable. As an old man, Plato set down an account of his youthful enthusiasm for political reform and his eventual disillusionment:

> *At last I saw that as far as all states now existing are con-cerned, they are all badly governed. For the condition of their laws is bad almost past cure, except for some mirac-ulous accident. So I was compelled to say, in praising true philosophy, that it was from it alone that one was able to discern all true justice, public and private. And so I said that the nations of men will never cease from trouble until either the true and genuine breed of philosophers shall come to political office or until . . . the rulers in the states shall by some divine ordinance take to the true pursuit of philosophy.*

As Socrates was, for Plato, the archetype of the philosopher, the model of justice and wisdom, so Socrates' conviction and sentencing to death by Athens was taken by him as evidence of the radical evil and injustice of the state. In memory of Socrates, and to avenge his death, Plato dedicated himself to the philosopher's quest for justice, wisdom, and truth. A man might choose to keep quiet and mind his own business, content to live a gracious life, careful to commit neither impiety nor injustice in a world that is both impious and unjust. This, Plato admits, would be no small achievement. For the philosopher, however, it is not enough. He must seek the ideal both on his own account and on that of society, "for in the state that fits him he himself will attain greater proportions and along with his private salvation will save the community as well." The philosopher, Plato seems to be saying, cannot see justice clearly if he does not see himself as the ruler of the state. Even if the idea of the philosopher-king is impractical as a concrete political goal, it may be the only way to arrive at the ideas of truth and justice.

Thucydides was concerned with the same problems of justice and power as Plato, but where Plato saw in the state justice "writ large," Thucydides saw only power. It was his purpose to assuage the conscience of Athens – not for the death of Socrates (which may have occurred only after Thucydides' own death), but for that other trial of conscience to which Athens was subjected, the Peloponnesian War. When Athens and Sparta, the freemen of Greece, together defeated the superior military forces of Persian despotism, Greece took its victory as the proper reward of justice. Succeeding events, however, shocked the Greek sense of moral propriety. The allies fell out, each coveting the other's empire, so that the struggle for freedom became a cynical struggle for power. Unlike previous and later empires, Athens scorned to resort to the dubious sanction of religion or a hypocritical concern for the welfare of its subjects.

In support of the fight against enemies abroad and dissidents at home, Thucydides invoked the idea of imperialism as the normal and natural behavior of states. "No one can be blamed," he has the Athenian envoys to Sparta say, shortly before the outbreak of the war, "with matters of the greatest consequence at stake, for disposing of the risks to his own best advantage." No nation is deterred by the argument of justice from pursuing its best interest, if it has the power to obtain that interest. The established rule of politics is that the liberty of the weaker is curtailed by the power of the stronger. Men rule whatever they can master. "We have not laid down this law nor were we the first to follow it when laid down; we but took it over, followed it, and will leave it after us, a thing already existing and destined to exist forever."

Athens, Thucydides reasoned, taught the world to regard power not as a means but as an end. As long as human nature remained the same, and there was every reason to suppose it would, men would lust after power for no better motive than the desire for power. Since this was the natural state of affairs, Thucydides concluded that it would be futile to will it otherwise. "Justice" was only one of the many "fair words" with which men adorned their speech, attempting to deceive the weak and stupid. Morality was but another name for the conventions that keep a society in order. Yet even Thucydides, the progenitor of Machiavelli and Hobbes, made his obeisance, after a fashion, to justice and morality. The Athenian envoys, arguing their case by proxy of the historian, contradict themselves by claiming first that they behaved exactly as any other people would have in a similar situation, and then that they behaved better than the others. In a few instances, describing, for example, the barbarous murder of the entire population of one small town, Thucydides permits himself the luxury of indulging in moral indignation. This is because evil was done wantonly, beyond the needs of the situation. When men are wicked by choice, Thucydides admits that moral comment is in order.

Those deserve praise who, while following the dictates of man's nature and ruling others, still prove juster than their own strength would warrant. At least, we think that if others took over our empire, they would have proved conclusively how moderate we are; yet in our case, thanks to our decent behavior, we have got a bad name rather than a good one, and this is most unreasonable.

The material of Thucydides' history is, to a remarkable extent, the material of present-day history. It is sometimes enough, particularly in the controversy between states (for "Athens vs. Sparta" one may read "America vs. Russia"), to put the moral argument in its most modest form, as Thucydides did. We have only done what had to be done; we have not killed as barbarians but as soldiers. Yet the concession to justice was greater than Thucydides intended. In denying that empires are governed by justice, he unwittingly affirmed the reality of something called justice, even though it is more often conspicuous by its absence than by its presence. For over two thousand years, if Athens and Thucydides are taken as the founders of "political realism," nations have violated every precept of justice, and there have been those who have solemnly read the idea out of existence. Yet neither the testimony of our senses nor the reasoning of our betters has succeeded in eliminating the consciousness of justice (and injustice) from our minds, or even in removing it from the highest position in political and moral philosophy.

"The extraordinary feature of the Athenian empire," Grene observes, "is that the Athenians built it with nothing to stand between themselves and the suffering and injustice they caused; that they faced it all together, every one of them, in individual moral responsibility all the time." "Suffering," "injustice," "moral responsibility": this may be at the opposite moral pole from Plato, but it is assuredly in the same mode of philosophical discourse.

———————

In a totally different universe of discourse is the kind of political thought to which the "moderns" are partial and which is currently known not as political philosophy but as political science. Political science is not content merely to give novel answers to the traditional problems of political philosophy. It denies the meaningfulness of the questions themselves. In keeping with the professions of "positive" science, it refuses to be distracted, by metaphysical and moral speculations, from the only meaningful task: the creation of a scientific, empirically grounded system of politics.

Between Thucydides and the political scientist there are obvious points of resemblance. Both pride themselves on their hardheaded, realistic confrontation of the facts of political life. Both see in power the basic, sometimes the only, fact of politics. Yet Thucydides is within the tradition of political philosophy while political science remains stubbornly outside of it. For Thucydides, the drama of politics comes from the necessity to be immoral. No matter how often justice is defeated, or how predictable its defeat may be, it is always a contender in the political arena; it exists to try men's consciences and provide the plots for tragedy. The political scientist, on the other hand, would like to know nothing of conscience or tragedy. To him, justice regarded as a moral abstraction or absolute is often little more than a feeble memory left over from the prescientific age of myths and heroes. Again, for Thucydides, the facts of life are hard, ineluctable, and man is a prisoner both of nature and of history. The political scientist, often an optimist by temperament, regards man as a plastic creature able to do with himself what he would, and history as a bad dream, which daylight brings to an end.

Power and Society: A Framework for Political Inquiry (1950) is the work of two of the ablest men in the field. Harold D. Lasswell of Yale is generally acknowledged to be the dean of political science in America, and Abraham Kaplan, a young philosopher at the University of California, Los Angeles, is a distinguished student of Rudolf Carnap, the logical positivist. As might be expected from such a collaboration, the book opens with a statement of the difference between political science and political philosophy. Political philosophy is generally taken to include two distinct categories: political science concerned with what is, political doctrine with what ought to be. Throughout this book, however, political philosophy is generally used as a synonym for political doctrine and in contradistinction to political science. Lasswell and Kaplan describe their own work as falling exclusively within the province of science.

There is more in this than a staking out of conflicting claims. Lasswell and Kaplan are less concerned with limiting their own sphere of operations than with eliminating their competitors. After assigning boundaries to science and philosophy, they proceed to cut the ground out from under the feet of philosophy. Political philosophy, it soon appears, is a not quite legitimate enterprise in this advanced age. Theories of "what ought to be," of the "right, good, and proper," are deemed to be somewhat disreputable, not a seemly preoccupation for the serious thinker, merely the expressions of men's prejudices and preference. They are ideologies intended to legitimize and justify political power in the eyes of the world, to act as a convenient façade behind which the realities of power can function undisturbed. The scientist, dispassionately observing the ways of men, uses these philosophies as case studies of what men believe, or think they believe. The philosophical doctrines of Plato are of no more validity or significance than the religious rites of the Australian aborigines or the voting habits of American citizens. Philosophy is informative the way lies are informative. It tells the scientist something about the pathology of the philosopher, but nothing about the objective nature of reality.

It is in keeping with this conception of political science that Lasswell and Kaplan take, as the subject matter of their study, the composition and distribution of "values" – values understood as the wealth, power, and prestige which men in a given society happen to seek. These values alone are deemed to be real. They can be seen, measured, tested, and assigned numerical quantities. The values of the philosopher, such as wisdom, truth, and justice, do not enter into the calculations of the scientist. In a previous work, *World Politics and Personal Insecurity* (1934), Lasswell described those spurious values as symbols of "ego insecurity" by means of which the individual seeks to relieve his psychic "tensions"; in the present they are the rationalizations that induce him to submit to authority. In either case, they are evasive and unsubstantial compared with the tangibles of wealth, power, and prestige.

There would be little point in quarreling with political science, as Lasswell and Kaplan understand it, were it not that political science, in their sense, is inimical to political philosophy in Strauss's sense. This is not true of all political scientists. There are those whose principles and purposes are more modestly empirical. The experts in public administration, regulation, and legislation perform a valuable function in amassing essential facts about the mundane workings of politics. Political philosophy does not deny the legitimacy of this kind of political science. Nor does this mode of political science infringe upon the domain of political philosophy. To accredit the study of urban and rural, or racial and sexual differences regarding party affiliation, pressure groups, or political influence is not to discredit the study of human nature and social justice, the relations of state and society, or the tensions between private and public morality.

Lasswell and Kaplan, to be sure, scorn to be mere collators of facts. On the contrary, against the "brute empiricists," they oppose a loftier conception of political science: "Of themselves, of course, 'facts' are mere collections of details; they are significant only as data for hypotheses" – hypotheses that elucidate the processes and activities implicit in political science. This might be a legitimate conception of political science and need not necessarily interfere with the inquiries of political philosophy. It only becomes a challenge to political philosophy when the hypotheses deny those of political philosophy, when "power" is treated as objective reality but "justice" is not, when "interests" are deemed an appropriate tool of political analysis and "morals" are not.

Science, it is often implied, is willing to sacrifice the amenities of civilization – sentiment, style, and moral indignation – upon the altar of truth. Truth is indeed worthy of the greatest sacrifices; but it would be tragic were the sacrifice to be in vain, were it to prove that what is sacrificed is truth itself. Consider the dilemma of the political scientist who has engaged to analyze one of the most distressing phenomena of our time, the concentration camp. Presumably, he would have to refrain from such obvious expressions of judgment as cruelty, inhumanity, barbarity, savagery, horror, atrocity, ignominy, degradation. Yet not to use these words, or their moral equivalents, would be to ignore the most important facts about the camps and to miss their significance in human history. To think of them in the judicial manner prescribed by political science is to think of them as the Nazis did. There could be no greater perversion of truth.

Fortunately, men, even political scientists, are generally less corrupt than their theories would make them. After all their warnings against the "normatively ambiguous" statements in which judgment creeps in to contaminate the purity of science, Lasswell and Kaplan themselves succumb to the human weakness of ambiguity. "Our own values," they confess, "are those of the citizen of a society that aspires toward freedom. Hence we have given special attention to the formulation of conditions favorable to the establishment and continuance of a free society." They hasten to add, however, that they are "not concerned with the justification of democratic values, their derivation from some metaphysical or moral base." Although the political philosopher may find it hard to conceive of anything more important for the establishment and continuance of a free society than the moral and metaphysical justification of democratic values, it is interesting to watch political science confronting, even on its own terms, the problem of freedom.

———

In the first great "Battle of the Books," in the seventeenth century, the moderns claimed to see farther than the ancients by standing on their shoulders. The moderns of today spurn such aids. Raising themselves by their own bootstraps, they hope to tower above centuries of thinking men. Leo Strauss, and the mode of political philosophy he represents, has us not only standing on the shoulders of the ancients but entering their heads and imbibing their spirit and their truths.

1951

CHAPTER TWO

William James:
Once-Born and Twice-Born

W E HAVE BEEN witnessing in recent years a vigorous and almost concerted resurgence of atheism. The writers Sam Harris, Richard Dawkins, Daniel Dennett, and Christopher Hitchens – the "Four Horsemen of the New Atheism," as they have characterized themselves – have advanced a particularly militant form of nonbelief. In best-selling books bearing such titles as *The End of Faith* (Harris, 2004), *The God Delusion* (Dawkins, 2006), *Breaking the Spell* (Dennett, 2006), and *God Is Not Great* (Hitchens, 2007), they have launched a full-fledged war against religion. The "God Hypothesis," they insist, is a scientific conjecture about the nature of the universe and must be judged as such, where it utterly fails. It cannot claim to be a necessary basis for morality, because morality is sufficiently accounted for on naturalistic and evolutionary grounds. Nor can it be justified by putting science and religion in separate spheres ("non-overlapping magisteria"), as the paleontologist Stephen Jay Gould proposed, with science presiding over the empirical realm and religion over the moral, because the two spheres are not distinct and science presides over both. For the four horsemen and their followers, religion, in whatever form, is both spurious and redundant.

Perhaps in response to the New Atheists (although he does not mention them by name), another self-proclaiming atheist has entered the debate with another provocatively titled book, *Religion for Atheists: A Non-Believer's Guide to the Uses of Religion* (2012). Alain de Botton does not attempt to refute religion; he simply stipulates that it is not true. It is, however, "sporadically useful, interesting, and consoling," and can therefore be enlisted in the service of atheists. For people trying to cope with the pains and difficulties of life, religions (not religion in the abstract but institutional religions) are "repositories" of goods that can assuage their ills. By appropriating those goods – "music, buildings, prayers, rituals, feasts," and the like – and introducing them into secular society, de Botton proposes to rescue that which is "beautiful, touching and wise" from religions that are no longer true and put it to use by an atheism that is indubitably true but sadly deficient in such consolations.

To anyone even casually familiar with the perennial debate between religion and science, both the New Atheism of the four horsemen and the "Neo-Atheism," as it might be dubbed, of de Botton seem peculiarly old-fashioned – retro, as we now say. And it is old-fashioned enough to recall a participant in that debate more than a century ago. The Harvard philosopher William James did not identify himself as an atheist. On the contrary, it was as a believer that he defended religion, but a believer of a special sort and a religion that the orthodox, then and now, would not recognize as such. If de Botton is a Neo-Atheist, James qualifies as a Neo-Believer.

James's 1896 lecture "The Will to Believe" was prompted, he said, by the "freethinking and indifference" he encountered at Harvard. He warned his audience that he would not offer either logical or theological arguments supporting the existence of God or any particular religion, ritual, or dogma. His "justification of faith" derived instead entirely from the "will" or the "right" to believe, to "adopt a believing attitude in religious matters, despite the fact that our merely logical intellect may not have been coerced." James knew this would not go down well with the students and philosophers in the eminent universities. To the obvious objection that denying the "logical intellect" is to give up any claim to truth, he replied that it is in defense of truth that faith is justified – the truth provided not by logic or science but by experience and reflection. Moral questions, he pointed out, cannot be resolved with the certitude that comes from objective logic or science. And so with religious faith:

> *When I look at the religious question as it really puts itself to concrete men, and when I think of all the possibilities which both practically and theoretically it involves, then this command that we shall put a stopper on our heart, instincts, and courage, and wait – acting of course meanwhile more or less as if religion were not true – till doomsday, or till such time as our intellect and senses working together may have raked in evidence enough – this command, I say, seems to me the queerest idol ever manufactured in the philosophic cave.*

This was James's response to the nonbelievers of his day. The will to believe, deriving from "our heart, instincts, and courage," "our passional and volitional nature," speaks with an authority, a truth, as compelling as that which science and logic provide in other realms of experience. "The heart," he quoted Pascal, "has its reasons of which reason knows nothing."

The popular reception accorded the publication of "The Will to Believe" – it was reprinted three times in its first year – inspired James to write a more ambitious series of lectures. Published in 1902, *The Varieties of Religious Experience* consists largely of case studies of different kinds of believers responding to different needs and natures. The varieties, ranging from the familiar to the mystical, the saintly and even the neurotic, belong to the "personal branch" of religion rather than the institutional. The common denominator is a sense of the "divine presence," the "supreme reality," "something larger than ourselves," the "higher part of the universe" identified as God. For the pragmatist – or "radical empiricist," as James described himself – this is theology enough. "God is real since he produces real effects."

Even more provocative than this personal, permissive view of religion is the theme that appears in the middle of the book and puts the whole of it in a different light. James quotes the English writer Francis Newman: "God has two families of children on this earth, the once-born and the twice-born." The once-born, in James's words, "see God, not as a strict Judge, not as a Glorious Potentate, but as the animating Spirit of a beautiful harmonious world, Beneficent and Kind, Merciful as well as Pure." They are not self-righteous, but they are romantic and complacent, because they make little of sin and suffering, of human imperfection and the "disordered world of man." Theirs is the religion of the "healthy-minded." Accompanying the advance of "so-called" liberalism in Christianity, it represents a victory over the old "morbid," "hell-fire theology." Far from dwelling on the sinfulness and depravity of man, the once-born belittle sin, deny eternal punishment, and insist

upon the dignity of man. "They look at the continual preoccupation of the old-fashioned Christian with the salvation of
his soul as something sickly and reprehensible rather than
admirable."

The twice-born, by contrast – the "sick souls" and "mor-
bid-minded" – are all too aware of the existence of evil, indeed,
of the "experience of evil as something essential." Where the
once-born look upon the "children of wrath" as "unmanly and
diseased," the twice-born look upon the "healthy-minded" as
"unspeakably blind and shallow."

On first reading, James would seem to weigh the argument
in favor of the once-born. Surely, "healthy" is more desirable
than "sickly," "dignity" more commendable than "depravity,"
and a "liberal" theology more enlightened than a "hell-fire"
one. James deliberately chose such harsh words to put the
issue in its boldest terms, to express the true irony of the
human condition. It is not long, however, before he intervenes
in the quarrel unequivocally on the side of the twice-born: "It
seems to me that we are bound to say that morbid-mindedness
ranges over the wider scale of experience." Healthy-minded-
ness is simply inadequate as a philosophical doctrine "because
the evil facts which it refuses positively to account for are a
genuine portion of reality; and they may after all be the best
key to life's significance, and possibly the only openers of our
eyes to the deepest levels of truth."

In a chapter with the promising title "The Divided Self,
and the Process of Its Unification," James suggests some reconciliation between the once-born and the twice-born. Human
beings, we are reminded, exhibit varieties and mixtures of each
outlook. Yet the duality remains. Happiness of a sort is not
denied to the twice-born; nor is religious peace. But theirs is a
complicated happiness and peace, not to be achieved by an

algebraic calculation of pluses and minuses. The real world is a "double-storied mystery" in which the pluses and minuses, good and evil, are inextricable and ineradicable. It is this world that the twice-born inhabits and understands. Toward the end of *Varieties*, James observes that "the outlook upon life of the twice-born – holding as it does more of the element of evil in solution – is the wider and completer."

Critics may well object that a religion based upon a will to believe can justify any kind of belief, however eccentric or even mischievous, and may question the viability of a faith indepen- dent of institutions, dogmas, and rituals. But they cannot deny the fact that something like a will to believe is the motivating force for many people who are distrustful of those institutions and skeptical of those dogmas and rituals but who neverthe- less feel a spiritual need and seek a faith responsive to their personal needs and passions. There is no doubt that James counted himself among the twice-born and experienced such a will to believe. As if testifying to his own faith, James wrote in his notes as he prepared the lectures that became *Varieties of Religious Experience*, "A man's religion is the deepest and wis- est thing in his life."

———

"A man's religion," but also a man's irreligion, James might have said. For the varieties of irreligion reflect the same once- born / twice-born dichotomy as the varieties of religion. The "New Atheists" easily fall into the category of the once-born, being as monolithic in their devotion to science as religious fundamentalists are in their monotheism. "Neo-Atheists," on the other hand, are aware of the psychological and spiritual deficiencies of atheism and eager to import into secular society some of the enduring "goods" of traditional religions. Thus, they exhibit more of the character of the twice-born. So too, current varieties of will-to-believers are of both types. "New Age" disciples, rejecting traditional religion and aspiring to personal fulfillment and universal harmony, belong to the once-born. "Born-again" Christians, though, are of a mixed variety. They are twice-born in their acute recognition of sin, which prompts some of them to return to traditional churches with their rituals and dogmas, while others seek refuge – like the once-born New-Agers – in transitory nondogmatic, nonritualistic churches or megachurches.

The more interesting challenge to the once-born / twice-born concept is traditional institutional religion. Only briefly, near the end of *Varieties*, does James venture into that realm. Citing John Henry Newman, the key figure in England's Catholic revival in the 1830s and 1840s, on the aesthetic appeal of Catholicism, James explains why Protestantism will not make many converts from Catholicism.

> *The latter [Catholicism] offers a so much richer pasturage and shade to the fancy, has so many cells with so many different kinds of honey, is so indulgent in its multiform appeals to human nature, that Protestantism will always show to Catholic eyes the almshouse physiognomy.... To intellectual Catholics many of the antiquated beliefs and practices to which the Church gives countenance are, if taken literally, as childish as they are to Protestants. But they are childish in the pleasing sense of "childlike" – innocent and amiable, and worthy to be smiled on in consideration of the undeveloped condition of the dear people's intellects. To the Protestant, on the contrary, they are childish in the sense of being idiotic falsehoods.*

23

He must stamp out their delicate and lovable redundancy, leaving the Catholic to shudder at his literalness. . . . The two will never understand each other – their centers of emotional energy are too different.

Although the words "once-born" and "twice-born" do not appear in this passage, they are implicit in it. The sophisticated, broad-minded Catholic, indulgent of the "multiform appeals to human nature," is surely of the twice-born type; the literal-minded Protestant who wants to stamp out those "redundancies" is closer to the once-born. The passage is all the more telling because it is, in one sense, counterintuitive. One might expect James, driven by a will to believe not satisfied by institutional religions, to be better disposed to the Protestant's criticism of those "antiquated beliefs and practices." Instead it is the wise and worldly Catholic's justification of them that he vigorously endorses.

It is regrettable that James does not extend his discussion to other institutional religions – to Judaism, most notably. The Old Testament is a case study of his theories. The Garden of Eden is the primordial story of the twice-born. Adam and Eve eat of the forbidden fruit, acquire the knowledge of good and bad, and experience the fatal loss of innocence and grace. In that one act, humanity is condemned to a life of misery, pain, and death. Yet despite the loss of innocence, as the rest of Genesis demonstrates, human beings go forward into the world with hope and longing for redemption. Genesis is, literally, the story of the genesis of the twice-born.

In the debate between religion and science, between believers and nonbelievers, the terrible simplifiers on both sides tend to dominate the discourse. Today the contenders have become more aggressive than ever – and more simplistic. This is why William James can speak to us with a special relevance and cogency. And he does so not in an affable spirit of compromise or conciliation but as a hardheaded realist – a twice-born, in short. If he was so appreciative of the varieties of religious experience, it is because he was so acutely aware of the varieties – and complexities, anomalies, and difficulties – of life itself. This may be James's legacy to us: the idea of the once-born and twice-born that illuminates so many of our controversies, not only about religion but about philosophy, politics, literature, and much else.

2012

The Past versus the Present

CHAPTER THREE

Burke's War on Terror – and Ours

———————— ❚❘❘❘❘❙ ————————

THE WAR ON TERROR is over, President Obama assured us
in 2013. A year later we were told that the war is very much
with us and will be pursued with all due diligence. The
president had obviously responded to polls reflecting public
disapproval of his policies, as well as to critics in his own party.
Dianne Feinstein, chairman of the Senate Intelligence Committee, sadly commented on Obama's admission that he had
"no strategy yet": "I think I've learned one thing about this
president, and that is: He's very cautious – maybe in this
instance too cautious."

Two centuries ago, in the midst of another "war on terror" –
or so he thought of it – Edmund Burke reproached his prime
minister for a similar failing. He had admired William Pitt for
his leadership in the war with France, but now, out of excessive
caution, Pitt was seeking peace with that "regicide" regime. In
his *Letters on a Regicide Peace*, Burke decried this effort as a
dangerous folly:

> *There is a courageous wisdom: there is also a false, reptile
> prudence, the result not of caution but of fear. Under*

misfortunes it often happens that the nerves of the under-
standing are so relaxed, the pressing peril of the hour so
completely confounds all the faculties, that no future
danger can be properly provided for, can be justly esti-
mated, can be so much as fully seen.

That false prudence was all the more serious in the case of a
"great state" like England, which needed to behave in a manner
commensurate with its power.

The rules and definitions of prudence can rarely be exact;
never universal. I do not deny that in small truckling states
a timely compromise with power has often been the means,
and the only means, of drawling out their puny existence;
but a great state is too much envied, too much dreaded, to
find safety in humiliation. To be secure, it must be
respected. Power, and eminence, and consideration, are
things not to be begged. They must be commanded: and
they who supplicate for mercy from others can never hope
for justice through themselves.

It is an odd argument to come from Burke, and perhaps the
more telling for that. If there is any one political principle associated with Burke, it is prudence. *Letters on a Regicide Peace*
was written in 1796. Five years earlier, in his *Appeal from the
New to the Old Whigs*, he had pronounced prudence the first of
all virtues. "Prudence is not only first in rank of the virtues,
political and moral, but she is the director, the regulator, the
standard of them all." But prudence was associated with a cor-
ollary principle, "circumstances," which determine what is
wise and prudent in any particular situation. On this occasion,

in a war with an implacable enemy, a misplaced prudence was not a virtue but a fatal flaw.

The war with France was such an occasion, Burke believed, because France was the consummate enemy, the very embodiment of terror. The idea of the "Reign of Terror" (*la Grande Terreur*) was not, as some have suggested, the invention of disaffected émigrés or hostile historians. "Terror" was the term the revolutionaries publicly and proudly applied to themselves. In December 1793, with the executions well under way (they amounted to thirty thousand or more in a two-year period), the "Constitution of the Terror" officially inaugurated the "Government of the Terror." Robespierre, the head of the Committee of Public Safety, explained why terror was the necessary instrument of the revolution – the "Republic of Virtue," as he saw it: "If the spring of popular government in time of peace is virtue, the springs of popular government in revolution are at once virtue and terror: virtue, without which terror is fatal; terror, without which virtue is powerless. Terror is nothing other than justice, prompt, severe, inflexible." (Robespierre was soon executed, becoming one of the notable victims of the Terror.)

Burke agreed with Robespierre about this, if about nothing else: There was a necessary connection between the revolution and terror, as there was between the Revolutionary Wars and terror. Burke's *Letters on a Regicide Peace* (like his *Reflections on the Revolution in France*) may be accused of hyperbole. But if his account of the "scourge and terror" of the Revolutionary Wars seems exaggerated, it would not be at all exaggerated if applied to the current wars waged by the Islamic State. Indeed, it is uncannily prescient. With only slight changes of wording, we can adapt and update Burke's tract.

"Out of the tomb of the murdered Monarchy in France [read: "Out of the womb of the murderous Islamic State"] has arisen a vast, tremendous, unformed spectre, in a far more terrific guise than any which ever yet have overpowered the imagination and subdued the fortitude of man." (One can also imagine the Islamic State, as it imposes sharia law upon its terrain, assuming for itself the title "Republic of Virtue.")

The French war was not only murderous, Burke contended, it was also "peculiar," and that made it all the more threatening.

We are in a war of a peculiar nature. It is not with an ordinary community, which is hostile or friendly as passion or as interest may veer about; not with a State which makes war through wantonness, and abandons it through lassitude. We are at war with a system, which, by its essence, is inimical to all other Governments, and which makes peace or war, as peace and war may best contribute to their subversion. It is with an armed doctrine that we are at war. It has, by its essence, a faction of opinion, and of interest, and of enthusiasm, in every country. To us it is a Colossus which bestrides our channel. It has one foot on a foreign shore, the other upon the British soil.

Burke's words can be echoed almost exactly today, for it is just such a peculiar war we are waging against just such a peculiar enemy. The Islamic State is not an ordinary state with which we can negotiate or compromise, not a "manageable problem" we can resolve gradually and temperately, but an "armed doctrine," a "system," a "faction of opinion," which knows no compromise and cannot be managed. With such an enemy, there cannot be a "red line" defining how far, and no further, we may go; a "no troops on the ground" policy limiting our involvement in the war; an "end-of-war" strategy that prescribes at the outset when and how the war will be terminated. On the contrary, a war with such an enemy is a total war – and, Burke insisted, a "*long* war" (his italics). "I speak it emphatically, and with a desire that it should be marked, in a *long* war; because, without such a war, no experience has yet told us, that a dangerous power has ever been reduced to measure or to reason." The purpose of the war must be nothing less than to "destroy that enemy" or it will "destroy all Europe"; and in order to destroy the enemy, "the force opposed to it should be made to bear some analogy and resemblance to the force and spirit which that system exerts."

Letters on a Regicide Peace, which appeared in October 1796 as a pamphlet containing two letters, was Burke's last published work. He died the following year. (Two other letters were published posthumously.) Burke had described himself to a friend as "a dejected old man, buried in an anticipated grave of a feeble old age, forgetting and forgotten in an obscure and melancholy retreat." *Letters on a Regicide Peace* gives no hint of that. It is as bold and vigorous as the *Reflections* – and it was surprisingly popular, considering the fact that Burke was urging upon England a long, dangerous, and costly war. The mood of the American public today, to judge by the polls, should be receptive to his message, understanding our war on terror as he understood his, and willing to pursue it with the commitment and energy it deserves.

2014

CHAPTER FOUR

Arnold's Culture War – and Ours

———————IIIII———————

IN THE "CULTURE WARS" currently being waged in the universities and the media, the very title of *Culture and Anarchy* has a combative ring. Matthew Arnold himself is often invoked as a partisan, if not as commander in chief, of the forces doing battle for "culture" and against "multiculturalism," culture being associated with the common heritage symbolized by the "Great Books" and "Western civilization," and multiculturalism with the distinctive cultures of classes, races, sexes, ethnic groups, and whatever other minorities are said to be "marginalized."

It was in another contentious period, the student "revolution" of 1968 – which happened to coincide with the one-hundredth anniversary of the appearance of Arnold's book – that I first introduced *Culture and Anarchy* to a graduate seminar. Then, too, it seemed peculiarly relevant, but for a different reason. The issue at that time was not so much culture as authority: the authority of the educational "establishment" most immediately, and authority in general. If Arnold is on the side of culture now, he was just as assuredly on the side of authority then.

Rereading the book today, one is aware of anomalies that

should give pause to both sides. It is these anomalies that make its republication, with commentaries by four distinguished critics – Samuel Lipman, Maurice Cowling, Gerald Graff, and Steven Marcus – a cultural event in its own right. *Culture and Anarchy* is unquestionably "politically incorrect." Indeed, it was politically incorrect when it first appeared – for conservatives, for liberals, and for radicals.

What Arnold meant by "culture" and "anarchy" is not what his contemporaries meant by those words, or what we mean by them. His culture is not the genteel culture of "belles-lettres" and "dead languages" that his critics mocked. Nor is it popular culture, as we now understand that term. Although it is rooted in classical culture, Arnold's culture looks forward rather than backward; it is a prescription for a common, progressive, universal culture that would elevate and unify all classes. This culture is nothing less than the study and the pursuit of "total perfection," "the best which has been thought and said in the world." It is inspired not merely by reason but by "right reason," the reason that comes from the "best self" rather than the "ordinary self." It seeks to cultivate the "free play" of thought, the "sheer desire to see things as they are." It is what Jonathan Swift, in *The Battle of the Books*, calls "sweetness and light," beauty and intelligence, the "two noblest of things" that together constitute "human perfection."

If this idea of culture seems to us (as it did to many of Arnold's contemporaries) almost unbearably high-minded, his idea of anarchy is only a little less so. Anarchy is "doing as one likes." Mill is never mentioned by name, but the allusion could not have escaped his readers, for it was only a few years earlier that Mill had defined liberty in precisely those terms. Arnold finds evidence of the insidious spirit of "social anarchy" in the Hyde Park riot of July 1866, a demonstration for electoral reform that turned disorderly when access to the park was prohibited. The mob, affirming "an Englishman's best and most blissful right of doing what he likes," proceeded to rob and beat bystanders, while the City of London alderman who also served as colonel of the militia refused to authorize his troops to interfere.

This image of social anarchy is so dramatic that it may overshadow the more important sense of anarchy as Arnold understands it: cultural anarchy, not only doing as one likes but thinking and speaking as one likes. In contrast to the "free play" of thought that Arnold identifies with culture, this kind of free thought is guided only by the will to freedom – by no "standard of excellence," no ideal of "perfection," no "paramount authority of right reason," no recognition of the "best self." To the liberal politician who finds the greatness of England in the right of every Englishman to "say what he likes," Arnold retorts that the aspirations of culture are satisfied only if "what men say, when they may say what they like, is worth saying, has good in it and more good than bad."

———————

So far, Arnold's "anarchy" is the obverse of Mill's "liberty." But it goes well beyond that, becoming an indictment not only of liberalism but of what Arnold calls "Hebraism." Indeed, the antithesis between "culture" and "anarchy" can only be understood in the context of the larger Arnoldian dichotomy of "Hellenism" and "Hebraism." "Hellenism" is culture: right reason, the study of perfection, the free play of mind, the desire to see things as they really are. "Hebraism" is anarchy – but a very peculiar kind of anarchy, because it is rooted in an overweening concern for morality, good conduct, obedience to scripture and law. It is not "social anarchy," but intellectual, cultural, and spiritual anarchy. If the governing principle of Hellenism is the "spontaneity of consciousness," that of Hebraism is the "strictness of conscience." Hellenism is "right thinking"; Hebraism is "right acting." Arnold concedes that both are necessary for the "totality of perfection." But he leaves no doubt that "the one thing needful" in his own day is more thought and less action, more knowing and less doing. "To act is easy," he quotes Goethe, "to think is hard."

Hebraism, in Arnold's lexicon, is a euphemism for nonconformism. It is not, as one might think, synonymous with religion or revelation, to which Hellenism is often counterposed. In fact, one religious institution, the Church of England, plays an essential role in Arnold's conception of culture and therefore in Hellenism. By combining the "will of God" with "right reason," Anglicanism succeeds in producing a religious establishment that is both temperate in doctrine and national in scope, thus fulfilling the individual's spiritual and social needs while liberating him for the pursuit of culture:

> *Instead of battling for his own private forms for expressing the inexpressible and defining the undefinable, a man takes those which have commended themselves most to the religious life of his nation; and while he may be sure that within those forms the religious side of his own nature may find its satisfaction, he has leisure and composure to satisfy other sides of his nature as well.*

Nonconformism, on the other hand, has neither the religious latitude nor the national character of Anglicanism. It is a "hole and corner religion," narrow, sectarian, literal-minded, proud in its dissenting role – "The Dissidence of Dissent and the

Protestantism of the Protestant religion," as the motto of one nonconformist journal put it. Because it is provincial and parochial, it has produced no man "of the highest spiritual significance." The only great nonconformists (Milton, Wesley) had been trained in the establishment. Roman Catholicism and Judaism can boast of such men, but that is because they themselves are establishments – not national establishments, to be sure, but cosmopolitan ones.

The Hebraic, or nonconformist, ethic is also antithetical to culture because it favors the external aspects of life, not only by emphasizing doing rather than thinking, but also by putting a high value on wealth, material comforts, technological progress, and bodily vigor. It is curious to read Arnold's veiled criticism of his father in his derogatory references to "Muscular Christianity" (a label often applied to Thomas Arnold) and his disparagement of field sports and exercise (which were cultivated so assiduously at Rugby under the mastership of the elder Arnold). Unlike the Greeks, Arnold explains, for whom exercise was intimately related to the idea of "complete human perfection and happiness," modern man has a mechanical attitude to sport and exercise, as he does to all human affairs, seeking salvation in the outward manifestations of conduct and action.

Hebraism, in short, is "philistinism," a term first popularized by Arnold. As the principle of nonconformism represents religious equality, so the principle of philistinism represents cultural equality. The middle class is quintessentially philistine, since it makes "everyman" the arbiter in business, in politics, in religion, and in mind. The aristocracy (the "barbarians," as Arnold calls them) provides no alternative to philistinism, since it, too, is concerned only with external things and is conspicuously lacking in ideas or spirit. ("One has often wondered whether upon the whole earth there is anything so unintelligent, so unapt to perceive how the world is really going, as an ordinary young Englishman of our upper class.") The philistine attitude spills over into the "populace," the working class, half of which already aspires to the condition of the middle class; the inevitable triumph of this class will only bring with it a new form of philistinism. The common denominator of all the classes is the philistine assumption that happiness consists in "doing what one's ordinary self likes"; they have different notions of what that self likes, but it is always the ordinary self that prevails. America is the philistine nation par excellence, with "the Barbarians quite left out, and the Populace nearly."

———

"I myself," Arnold declares, "am properly a Philistine," that is, a member of the middle class. But he is middle-class with a difference. Indeed, all the classes have something of each other in them, and all of them have "aliens," independent spirits like Arnold himself, who are distinguished not by their class spirit but by a "general humane spirit," a "curiosity about their best self," and a "love of human perfection." These aliens are the bearers of culture. They, too, need encouragement from without, a "source of authority" not only in their own best selves but also in the world. In England that authority is found in two institutions: the established church and the state.

Arnold professes to be a liberal: "I am a liberal, yet I am a liberal tempered by experience, reflection and renouncement, and I am, above all, a believer in culture." So tempered is his liberalism that few liberals of his time (and fewer still of ours) would recognize him as one of their own. If Arnold had not already offended them with his criticism of "doing as one likes," and even of saying and thinking as one likes, his views on church and state would put him outside the pale. For he defends the church establishment more vigorously than most liberals (with the notable exception of Gladstone), and he associates that establishment with a state whose authority goes far beyond what any liberal (including Gladstone) would tolerate.

The state, as Arnold sees it, is not only a bulwark against anarchy. It is also the mainstay of culture:

> *Thus, in our eyes, the very framework and exterior order of the State, is sacred; and culture is the most resolute enemy of anarchy, because of the great hopes and designs for the State which culture teaches us to nourish. But as, believing in right reason, and having faith in the progress of humanity towards perfection and ever laboring for this end, we grow to have clearer sight of the ideas of right reason, and of the elements and helps of perfection, and as we come gradually to fill the framework of the State with them, to fashion its internal composition and all its laws and institutions conformably to them, and to make the State more and more the expression, as we say, of our best self, which is not manifold, and vulgar, and unstable, and contentious and ever-varying, but one, and noble, and secure, and peaceful and the same for all mankind, – with what aversion shall we not then regard anarchy, with what firmness shall we not check it, when there is so much that is so precious which it will endanger!*

If it is true, as is generally believed, that Arnold never read Hegel, it is all the more remarkable that he should have produced so perfectly Hegelian a view of the state – and so "politically incorrect" a view, "incorrect" for the England of his day as much as the America of ours, and for conservatives as much as liberals.

What, then, can one make of this "alien" thinker today? What is the relevance of *Culture and Anarchy* for our time?

———

The commentators in the new edition address just this question. The three Americans – Steven Marcus, Gerald Graff, and Samuel Lipman – focus on the issue of multiculturalism, which has emerged so prominently in this country in recent years. As if in direct rebuttal to Arnold, multiculturalism insists that there is no unifying "culture," no "right reason" or "best self," no idea of "perfection." Instead, every ethnic, racial, sexual, and social group produces its own cultural forms and distinctive "values," all of which are deemed to be equally valid and compelling. Any attempt to impose or even to encourage a "hegemonic" culture, let alone one supported by a religious establishment or, worse yet, the state itself, is "totalizing" and "totalitarian."

Multiculturalism is thus precisely the antithesis of Arnold's "culture" and the epitome of Arnold's "anarchy." It is, he would have said, "the Dissidence of Dissent," the exemplar of provinciality and parochialism, the triumph of the "ordinary self" over the "best self" – a best self "which is not manifold, and vulgar, and unstable, and contentious and ever-varying, but one, and noble, and secure, and peaceful and the same for all mankind."

On this issue Marcus and Lipman, whatever other reservations they have about Arnold, are in agreement with him. Marcus is not convinced by Arnold's attempt to displace religious belief by some "protean conception of culture," nor by his assignment to the state of the role of culture-bearer for the nation. But he does find Arnold's description of nineteenth-

century British nonconformism reminiscent of the multiculturalism of our own time, and his conception of culture a
valuable antidote to the divisive tendencies in our own society.
"This is the social idea," he quotes Arnold, "and the men of
culture are the true apostles of equality," for it is they who carry
"from one end of society to the other, the best knowledge of
their time ... to humanize it, to make it efficient outside the
clique of the cultivated and the learned, yet still remaining the
best knowledge and thought of the time."

Lipman quotes the same passage, commending Arnold for
his implicit criticism not only of multiculturalism – that
"anthropological omnium-gatherum" of cultures – but also of
the degraded popular culture of our day. Just as Arnold's culture unites and humanizes all classes, so our popular culture
brutalizes and depraves them, "rich and poor, white and black,
young and old." Arnold, Lipman allows, misconstrued the
nature of the state; he did not see that it contained within itself
the seeds of "monstrous tyranny." He also overestimated the
power of the religious and educational establishments to build
a "social consensus." But in his understanding of culture and
anarchy and his appreciation of the connection between culture and conduct, he has earned "a secure place for himself in
Western civilization."

If Arnold is the apostle of culture, Gerald Graff might be
said to be the apostle of anarchy, at least in Arnold's sense of
that term. Graff's quarrel with Arnold is not only on the subject of culture, but even more on the subject of reason. Arnold's
reason, he points out, is not rational in the philosophical sense;
it is not the reason of Aristotle, Descartes, or Kant. Nor is his
reason the free play of consciousness that he professes to
believe in, because that would jeopardize his notion of a common culture. It is the multiculturalist, Graff suggests, who has

the better claim to reason, because it is he who subjects the dominant culture to critical inquiry, whereas Arnold merely identifies culture with an establishment, which is an unreasoned tradition. As for the common culture that Arnold espouses, that too is illusive, for in a democracy the common culture can only be a "common debate over culture." Arnold's great mistake was his inability to imagine "a vital culture whose citizens simply agree to disagree about religion, art, philosophy, morality and politics."

This is an interesting argument, but not a persuasive one. If Arnold was unable to imagine a "common culture" that has nothing in common, where people disagree about virtually everything of importance in the life of the individual and of the community – religion, art, philosophy, morality, politics – others may have the same difficulty. To agree to disagree is surely an essential part of a common culture, but it can hardly be the whole; it may be a recipe for tribal coexistence (or tribal warfare, in which the agreement concerns only the rules of warfare), but not for a stable, healthy, vigorous society. Nor is Graff's appropriation of "reason" more conclusive, for an important strain of "cultural radicalism," as he acknowledges – and of multiculturalism in particular – is the denial of reason in the ordinary sense, let alone anything like Arnold's "right reason." Reason, or "linear logic" as it is derogatorily called, is said to be the product of the "hegemonic," "patriarchal," "Eurocentric" culture. This view of reason is at the heart of the multiculturalist critique of Western culture.

Maurice Cowling, the only English contributor to the volume, has a different quarrel with Arnold. He concedes that Arnold may be a valuable corrective to American academic and political idiosyncrasies, but he warns against consecrating him as an apostle of conservativism. For Arnold had a fatal flaw: a conception of religion that is faulty in itself and that is inconsistent with a truly conservative sense of politics, morals, and culture. Arnold may have intended to reconstruct religion so that it would become a vital part of modern culture, "but the sap which seeps out of an author is as important as the intention, and the sap which seeps out of Arnold is a sap which sucks out of Christianity almost everything that has been distinctive about it."

Drawing largely upon Arnold's other writings, Cowling concludes that the effect of his teaching is not to revivify Christianity by purging it of nonconformist parochialism, but to enervate it by treating the Bible as literature, and by making the Church of England an instrument for national unity in the vain hope of bringing the working classes "within the pale of the religious constitution." Culture's role is, in effect, to "translate theology" into cultural and social terms. In the course of that translation, however, little remains of "orthodox, historic, dogmatic, theological Christianity." And even less is left of the original purpose of the enterprise, for "Arnoldianism," in England at least, has become the creed of the university-educated classes. Far from promoting social solidarity, it has proved to be socially divisive, creating an "anti-populist high-minded 'correctness'" that is essentially "unconservative." In the name of true conservativism, Cowling concludes by giving Arnold not three, not even two, but only one and a half cheers.

It is curious that none of the commentators with the exception of Lipman raises another issue that may cause a liberal, as much as a conservative, to withhold a cheer or two from Arnold; and Lipman, while broaching the subject, does not see it as a problem. Toward the end of his essay, he quotes a passage from the preface to *Culture and Anarchy* in which Arnold pays tribute to "the habits and discipline received from Hebraism which remain for our race an eternal possession." Lipman concludes that this is why the book is so relevant today: it shows "the integral connection between culture and conduct," between "the mental life and the moral life." But that is certainly not the main thrust of the book. On the contrary, Arnold's insistent theme is the opposition between culture and conduct, between the mental life and the moral life, between Hellenism and Hebraism.

A passage in *Culture and Anarchy* suggests a possible reconciliation of these opposing forces. Is it not, Arnold asks, the just reward of the "long discipline of Hebraism" that "in the fullness of time ... man's two great natural forces, Hebraism and Hellenism, should no longer be dissociated and rival, but should be a joint force of right thinking and strong doing to carry him on towards perfection?" But that is in the fullness of time. In the here and now, for Arnold as for the present-day reader of his book, the message is not the conjunction or even the compatibility of Hebraism and Hellenism; it is their disjunction and their incompatibility, with Arnold himself serving as a passionate defender of Hellenism and a harsh critic of Hebraism. Moreover, Hebraism is faulted for its moralism as much as its materialism, for the "strictness of conscience" that inhibits, if it does not altogether prevent, the "spontaneity of consciousness" that is the glory of Hellenism.

There has been much discussion about this antithesis of Hebraism and Hellenism: whether it reflects an animus toward Judaism over and above that displayed toward nonconformism; whether Christianity itself, and not merely nonconformism, is implicated in the critique of Hebraism; and whether Arnold's conception of either Hebraism or Hellenism corresponds to the historical reality. The more urgent question for us, however, is the one that Arnold himself asked. What is "the one thing needful"? Is it a greater dose of Hellenism or of Hebraism, of consciousness or of conscience?

Much of the present appeal of Arnold, to those unfashionable souls who find him appealing, derives from his stance in the "culture wars." He is clearly on the side of what for shorthand purposes has been called the "canon": the idea that there is such a thing as Great Books ("the best which has been thought and said"), and that those books transcend the bounds of race, class, and gender. It should also be said that for Arnold, as for his latter-day admirers, that canon is subject to revision and expansion. This is implicit, after all, in his notion of "play of mind."

But some of his appeal also comes from a misunderstanding of his idea of anarchy. We take him to mean by anarchy what we mean by it: crime, violence, incivility, immorality – the "externals" of conduct and behavior that Arnold surely deplores (as in the case of the Hyde Park riot). But his anarchy is much broader than this kind of disorder and misconduct. It is Hebraism itself, the overweening concern for "right acting" rather than "right thinking," for "conscience" rather than "consciousness," that he regards as anarchic because it denies the superior claims of culture. In his terms, those who think that one of the major problems of our time is the moral disarray of society are as guilty of Hebraism and philistinism as the most dissenting of dissenting ministers.

———

If Arnold was so enthusiastic a Hellenist, it was perhaps because he was so much a Victorian. Like all good Victorians, he was able to rebel against Victorianism, secure in the knowledge that Victorian society was firm enough to withstand his rebellion. It was thus that Mill, who had a thoroughly conventional, even puritanical view of morality (and of sexual morality particularly), could take so radical a view of liberty and individuality, professing to welcome "experiments in living" and encouraging people to act upon their "personal impulses and preferences," their "eccentricities" and "peculiarities." He did so in the assurance that those experiments and eccentricities would not go beyond common "decency," or if they did, they would be properly suppressed and punished. Similarly, Arnold, himself the most proper of Victorians, could take so broad-minded a view of Hellenism and so narrow-minded a view of Hebraism, confident that society would continue to sustain the Hebraic "discipline" that made for a moral, civil, law-abiding community.

Toward the end of the preface of *Culture and Anarchy* (written after the chapters had appeared serially in the *Cornhill Magazine*), Arnold encapsulated his message about "the one thing needful": "Now, and for us, it is a time to Hellenize, and to praise knowing; for we have Hebraized too much, and have overvalued doing." He then added, as if anticipating the obvious criticism: "But the habits and discipline received from Hebraism remain for our race an eternal possession; and, as humanity is constituted, one must never assign them the second rank today, without being ready to restore them to the first rank tomorrow."

Tomorrow, some of us would say, is today. We might even suspect that were Arnold alive today, he might agree that if ever there was a time to restore those Hebraic habits and discipline to the "first rank," it is now. For we are confronted not with one thing needful, but with two things needful. If Hellenism is a corrective to the cultural anarchy of our time, Hebraism is just as surely a corrective to the moral and social anarchy. Now more than ever we can see that the two are not only compatible, they are inseparable.

1994

CHAPTER FIVE

Bagehot's Constitution – and Ours

WALTER BAGEHOT (1826–1877), "the greatest Victorian," as G. M. Young (himself a great historian of that period) memorialized him – editor of the *Economist*, author of *The English Constitution*, and a prolific essayist – is almost unknown today. (Even the pronunciation of his name is unfamiliar; it rhymes with gadget.) The publication of his *Memoirs*, dated October 1, 1876 (six months before his death), and signed by the author with the request that it not be released until after he died, is surely a great coup, an invaluable addition to the fifteen volumes (or eleven in other editions) of his collected works.

Well, not quite. The title page bears a less familiar name, Frank Prochaska, and the foreword reveals that *The Memoirs of Walter Bagehot* are not by Bagehot, and not edited by Prochaska, but written by Prochaska himself. Fictionalized memoirs – a red flag to a pedant like myself. Prochaska explains that he chose to write about Bagehot in the first person in the hope of portraying his life and mind more vividly than he could have done in a conventional biography. The pseudo-Bagehot is indeed vivacious. Yet the pedant in me regrets the absence of quotation marks and footnotes attesting to the real Bagehot. I supplied some of them by tracking down the sources and was pleased to find that the book consists, in large part, of long, almost verbatim extracts from Bagehot's writings. If the *Memoirs* cannot be appended to the collected works, they can serve as a brief and eminently readable introduction to a stimulating writer and thinker, a man for whom the term "public intellectual" may have been coined.

The book reminds us that it is not a psychoanalytically obsessed biographer but Bagehot himself who found in his personal life the source of his distinctive character and mind. He must have been thinking of himself when he described St. Paul as a "divided nature." He came by that nature honestly, genetically, so to speak. From his banker-father, reserved and austere, and his mother, "by turns gay and distraught," he inherited the "hybrid sensibility" that persisted throughout his life, permitting him to indulge the love of poetry and literature acquired from his mother while exercising the boldness and rigor of mind of his father. It was to his "divided nature" that Bagehot attributed his ability to retain equanimity while coping with the "dark realities" of life.

Those realities were dark indeed. His mother, to whom he was deeply attached, lived in varying stages of insanity much of her (and his) life. (Not mentioned in the *Memoirs* is his half brother, who was feeble-minded.) "Every trouble in life," he once remarked, "is a joke compared to madness." It is no wonder that Bagehot, like his mother, was subject to "bouts of melancholy" and that his "melancholy search for truth" intensified his "qualms about human motive and precipitous action." This lifelong experience (both his mother and his half brother predeceased him by only a few years) colored the whole of his life. "We see but one aspect of our neighbor," he wrote, "as we see but one side of the moon; in either case there is also a dark half, which is unknown to us. We all come down to dinner, but each has a room to himself." That aphorism is reflected in much that Bagehot did and thought, about political and social as well as private life. There is always a dark side, an unknown, perhaps irrational and unconscious side that has to be taken into account.

After graduating from college (University College London, not Oxford as his mother would have preferred, because his father objected to its religious requirement), Bagehot started the study of law, but found it uncongenial – starving, he complained, his "higher half thoughts, half instincts." A visit to Oxford acquainted him with the followers of John Henry Newman and prompted him to read and admire the man, although not to agree with him. Reflecting on the division in his own life between his mother's Anglicanism and his father's Unitarianism, Bagehot came to a view of religion that transcended any doctrinal creed: "In religious matters, it is prudent to venerate what we do not comprehend. . . . We cannot prove that God is infinite, omnipotent and good, but we require the assumption that He is so or all is dark." "Despite my doubting temper," he concluded, "I sought a rational, consoling creed."

Another visit, this time to Paris, brought to the fore the political side of his "doubting temper." He went there in 1851, at the age of twenty-five, just in time to witness the coup d'état of Louis-Napoleon and report upon it in a series of articles for the *Inquirer*, a Unitarian weekly. In a mood that might be interpreted, he confessed, as "satiric playfulness," even "cynicism," he proceeded to shock his "high-minded" liberal readers by defending the coup. "I am pleased to have seen a revolution, but once is enough," he told them.

That "revolution" turned out to be for the young Bagehot

what the momentous French Revolution was for Edmund Burke, moving him to entertain ideas that were at odds not only with those of his friends but with those of most of his countrymen. Unlike Burke, however, Bagehot approved of the revolution he observed. "The first duty of society is the preservation of society," he reminded his readers. In the face of a threatening social anarchy, Napoleon was justified in taking over the government and asserting a strong executive power tantamount to dictatorship.

Almost apologetically, Bagehot introduced another theme to account for the coup: "national character ... the least changeable thing in this ever-changeful world." It was the distinctive national characters of the two countries that made French politics so volatile and the English so stable. It was at this point that Bagehot "provocatively," as he said, used the word "stupidity" to explain the character of the English people and thus the stability of their regime:

> *The most essential mental quality for a free people whose liberty is to be progressive, permanent, and on a large scale, is what I provocatively call stupidity.... Stupidity [is] the roundabout common sense and dull custom that steers the opinion of most men.... Nations, just as individuals, may be too clever to be practical, and not dull enough to be free. Dullness is the English line, as cleverness is that of the French.*

Many years later, expressed somewhat more delicately, but still provocatively, this was to be one of the leading themes of *The English Constitution*.

Returning from Paris, Bagehot took a position in his father's bank, a three- or four-day-a-week job that he performed dutifully but unenthusiastically and that permitted him to devote his "spare mind," as he said, to writing: "Variety is my taste, and versatility my weakness." In essays about politicians and historians, poets and philosophers, he revealed his ironic sensibility and subtlety. Robert Peel was "a man of common opinions and uncommon abilities, who understands our real public opinion." Lord Palmerston was "not a common man, but a common man might have been cut out of him." Gibbon's history exemplified the "masculine tone" of the age, when men "ceased to write for students, and had not begun to write for women." Macaulay's mind was "eminently gifted" but unfortunately wanting in the necessary "uncertainties" and "gradations of doubt." Burke had been a great man with "the highest gifts of abstract genius," but for him "great ideas were a supernatural burden, a superincumbent inspiration." Wordsworth described "the world as we know it," while Shelley described "not our world, but that which is common to all worlds – the Platonic idea of a world." These are not merely clever aphorisms. They go to the heart of each man and of his work.

———

Bagehot's marriage in 1858 to Eliza Wilson, daughter of James Wilson, the editor of the *Economist*, brought him into another world. Urged by his mother to marry, he had flightily responded, "A man's mother is his misfortune, but his wife is his fault." In fact, his marriage was a happy one, Eliza and her cheerful sisters providing a satisfying "mixture of chaff and currency ... sense and nonsense ... the medley of great things and little, of things mundane and things celestial," which appealed to his double nature. With the death of James Wilson two years later, Bagehot succeeded him as editor of the *Economist*.

The editor of the *Economist* – or at least this editor – was occupied with subjects other than economics. One of the issues that dominated public discourse was the movement for parliamentary reform. The Reform Act of 1832 had given the suffrage to much of the middle classes, and Bagehot saw this in retrospect as a mixed good. But a new bill, proposing to extend the suffrage much further, was altogether bad. The "admirable dullness" of English government was giving way to the passions of theorists who, invoking doctrines of equality and natural rights, would give power to people unfit for power.

The "fitness to govern" was not an absolute quality adhering to every individual. "That fitness is relative and comparative; it must depend on the community to be governed and on the merit of other persons who may be capable of governing that community." In mid-nineteenth-century English society, that capability resided, for the most part, in the well-educated rather than the poorly educated. "Justice," Bagehot concluded, "is on the side of a graduated rule, in which all persons should have an influence proportionate to their political capacity."

The other great public affair confronting Bagehot was the American Civil War. Again, it was the absolutist nature of the issue that exercised him. He was as opposed to slavery as the abolitionists, he insisted, but was "less than sanguine" about the "easy eradication of such an entrenched institution." A negotiated agreement declaring the independence of the Southern states would have limited the extent of slavery and led naturally to its decline. What was fatal was the North's insistence upon the Union, a union sanctified by a constitution regarded as providential, carrying the moral weight of a religious doctrine.

Critical of Abraham Lincoln during the war, Bagehot came to admire him toward the end. After the assassination, he paid a moving tribute to him: "It took a President of genius to over-come the imperfections of the very Constitution to which he swore an oath.... We do not know in history another such example of the growth of a ruler in wisdom as he exhibited." But about the Civil War itself and the American Constitution, Bagehot remained firm. The war was unnecessary and the Constitution deeply flawed. "A rigid document unsuited to changing social conditions," it was incapable of coping with any crisis, least of all one so acute as the crisis over slavery.

———

It was against the background of those two constitutional cri-ses – the American Civil War and the campaign for parliamen-tary reform at home – that Bagehot wrote the book for which he is now best known, *The English Constitution*. Originally a series of articles, it was published in book form early in 1867, shortly before the passage of the Second Reform Act, which broadened the franchise still further. The title itself is anoma-lous. In view of his criticism of that "rigid document," the American Constitution, one might have expected Bagehot to argue that England, in her wisdom, did not have a constitution, still less a capitalized "Constitution" (as the word appears throughout his book). Instead, this constitutional "skeptic," as he described himself, redefined the idea of a constitution:

> *The English Constitution, though a source of useful polit-ical habits, is a mass of fictions that usefully disguise inconsistent practices, an ingenious hypocrisy with an array of outmoded relics on the surface and an efficient modern machine below. It is not a cathedral of government constructed by English genius, but the work of a careless*

race which captures the imagination of the ignorant and satisfies the reason of the educated.

Much of *The English Constitution* is an implicit, sometimes explicit, critique of the American Constitution, particularly of the separation of powers, which belies the "sovereign authority" required of government even in the ordinary course of events, let alone in critical times like that of the Civil War. England has something resembling this separation of powers in its three branches of government – king, Lords, and Commons. But the reality is different: a government comprising two parts, the "dignified" and the "efficient," working together in harmony. It is this "double government," a "disguised republic," that is the genius of the English constitution. And it is the monarch, the visible head of the dignified part of government, who sustains the disguised republic. "We have made, or rather, stumbled on, a marvel of intelligible government, which superimposes the poetry of monarchy upon a burgeoning democracy."

The term "stupid people" does not appear here, as it did in Bagehot's account of the Napoleonic coup, but the concept does. It is the "ignorant," "simple" people, the "lower orders" and "common folk," the "unthinking mass of common people" who appreciate the "poetry of monarchy," revering the queen and respecting her authority. And they do so not because it is in their best interest, but because she appeals to their higher instincts, elevating them above the mundane conditions of their lives. By the same token, these people respect, even revere, the "dull, traditional habit of mankind," the customs and beliefs that govern their public as well as personal lives. "Other things being equal, yesterday's institutions are by far the best for today; they are the most ready, the most influential, the most easy to get obeyed, the most likely to retain the reverence to which they alone inherit, and which every other must win." To be sure, the world changes, and with it the efficient parts of the government – which is how "a republic has insinuated itself beneath the folds of Monarchy."

A second edition of *The English Constitution*, released five years later, permitted Bagehot to rethink some of his judgments – about the Second Reform Act, for example. While reaffirming his objections to the act itself and his qualms about the "ignorant multitude" that made up the new electorate, he observed that even if there had not been such an act, succeeding generations would have brought about changes in society and thus in politics: "A political country is like an American forest: you have only to cut down the old trees, and immediately new ones come up to replace them."

In another article, he went so far as to propose the enfranchisement of women on the same basis as men: "It would have removed an anomaly in our electoral system and the balance of probabilities was that it would have done some good by bringing a wholly fresh element into political life." In the same spirit, he supported the granting of university degrees to women: "The frivolity of women is one of the greatest causes of vice and frivolity in men. If we can but have a generation of women somewhat less dull, and somewhat less inclined to devote themselves to silly occupations, we hope that not only their children but their husbands and brothers will be the gainers."

Bagehot had always been tempted to become an active participant in politics rather than a mere reporter, "albeit calmed," he typically added, "by a measure of ironic distance." While writing *The English Constitution*, and encouraged by William

Gladstone and others in the Liberal Party, he made two attempts to stand for Parliament, both unsuccessful – for good reason, as he had publicly expressed a want of faith in the "unlettered elector" whose vote he was now seeking. He once described himself as a historian *manqué*, and so he was a politician *manqué*.

> *For a man of doubting temper, hesitant to adopt a creed, suspicious of haste and ardent for moderation, a career in today's politics, however agreeable to one's self-esteem, is fraught with difficulty. I am a moderate Liberal, rather between sizes in politics – too conservative for many Liberals and too liberal for many Tories. A want of faith in political action is unusual in Parliament today, and I am wanting in zeal.*

Bagehot may have been wanting in zeal, but not in intellectual curiosity. Soon after the publication of *The English Constitution*, he embarked upon quite a different subject. Inspired by Charles Darwin, Herbert Spencer, and others, *Physics and Politics* (1872) described the progress of society from the "yoke of custom" to the "age of discussion," from the "age of status" to the "age of choice." Just as the physical world evolved by a process of natural selection, so did the political world, calling upon all the social, psychological, and material resources of mankind. And just as the evolution of species depended on individual and group traits, so the evolution of the polity depended on national character. Bagehot did not conceal his conviction that England, by virtue of its national character, was the end product of this process, its unique quality of "animated moderation" giving it an energy and balance of mind superior to all other nations, permitting it to sustain a "government by discussion," a "free government."

In all of his "variety and versatility," Bagehot never lost his interest in economics. One of his earliest articles, written in 1848 at the age of twenty-two, was "The Currency Monopoly"; this was followed four years later by "Money and Morals." A long series of articles on banking appeared in the *Saturday Review* and the *Economist*, and his last book, *Lombard Street* (1873), was on the money market and banking system. Two memorable essays on Adam Smith, marking the occasion of the anniversary of *The Wealth of Nations*, appeared in 1876, the year before Bagehot's death. These writings reflected the same practical, temperate, meliorative spirit, "a suspicion of abstract speculations in commerce," as in all affairs. "Ideologies," he insisted, "can be dangerous things." On the much-disputed subject of the Bank of England, for example, he recognized its faults but proposed to deal with them not, as some recommended, by abolishing the bank, but with "remedies" and "palliatives."

Bagehot also cautioned against making an ideology of laissez-faire. Although he shared many of the views associated with that doctrine, he did so with reservations and qualifications: "I do not belong to that uncompromising tribe of economists who condemn the intervention of government in the nation's business as a heinous crime and contrary to reason, for in an economic crisis the government has a duty to intervene in the national interest." Above all, he warned against equating economics with the totality of life and reducing man to the level of an economic being.

Economics, dealing with matters of business, assumes that man is actuated only by motives of business. It assumes that every man who makes anything, makes it for money, that he always makes that which brings him in most at least cost ... that every man who buys, buys with his whole heart, and that he who sells, sells with his whole heart, each wanting to gain all possible advantage. Of course, we know that men are not like this, but we assume it for simplicity's sake, as a hypothesis.

"Liberated from the 'siege of the social sciences,'" from academics and theorists, political economy could then be restored to "the real world inhabited by real men, men who are moral beings even as they engage in the business of buying and selling."

The title of the final chapter of the *Memoirs* may be a misnomer. "Valedictory" is too triumphal. The memoirist, true to his divided nature, is more cautious, more tentative.

My nomadic mind has never settled on a single subject; waiting for truth to come, I have followed the truth that came my way. My moderate Liberalism shrinks from difficult dogma and imperious superstition, from facile abstraction and precipitous action. It has more to do with tolerance, steady judgment and genial enjoyment than advocacy or creed.... I have sought to encourage a greater communion between literature and commerce; to restrain our reckless enterprise through culture and common sense; to give expression to a philosophy of equanimity; to translate the truths discovered by the dead into the language of the living.

Bagehot is his own best critic. If fault may be found with him, it is because he sometimes seemed to betray his own principles and go against the grain of his own temper. Why was he so adamant about excluding the "stupid people" from Parliament – the people who had the common sense, sound instincts, and respect for tradition that made them so supportive of the monarchy, the "dignified" part of government that was the necessary complement to the "efficient" part? And why, having made "stupidity" the unique virtue of the English people, "the most essential mental quality for a free people," did he feel it necessary, after the passage of the Second Reform Act, to take up the call of "Educate! Educate! Educate!"? On other occasions, he disparaged the educated classes as being too prone to theorize and generalize, to mistake abstractions for realities.

Bagehot confessed to being "between sizes in politics." But perhaps he was not sufficiently between sizes. He might have taken a lesson from the Conservative Benjamin Disraeli, who supported the Second Reform Act – indeed, almost any reform – because he had confidence in his own party as the "national party," and in the people, who were naturally conservative. Bagehot might also have been more appreciative of Disraeli's interventionist and imperialistic foreign policies and less enthusiastic for Gladstone's "little Englandism," which was wary of Europe and distrustful of the British Empire. He might have regarded the empire – the very idea of an empire – like the monarchy, as elevating the nation, giving it a purpose and dignity lacking in an isolated, insulated England.

On America, too, Bagehot may be faulted for not being faithful to himself. Why did he deny to the American Constitution the "anomalies" he so readily granted the English? The principle of the separation of powers did not deny, as he thought, the "sovereign authority" of government. The federal system provided the kind of dual loyalties that were akin to the Englishman's king and Parliament. And the country emerged from the Civil War with the Union, the United States of America, intact. Yet these criticisms, and others one might cite, have the effect of confirming Bagehot's wisdom, for it is he who provides the grounds for them.

———

A biography of Bagehot might well be entitled *The Wit and Wisdom of Walter Bagehot*. Commenting once on the frequent quotation of a sentence from *The English Constitution*, "We must not let daylight in upon magic," Bagehot remarked: "Am I to be remembered, like a Frenchman, simply for *bon mots*?" There are not many authors, French or English, whose collected works contain separate indexes of "Epigrams." In Bagehot, wit and wisdom are one and the same. "*Bon mots*" and "epigrams" hardly do justice to such gems as his pronouncement that "taken as a whole, the universe is absurd":

> *How can a merchant be a soul? What relation to an immortal being has the price of linseed or the brokerage on hemp? Can an undying creature debit petty expenses and charge for carriage paid? The soul ties its shoes; the mind washes its hands in a basin. All is incongruous.*

Or his comment on the professional writer who read and wrote without thinking or feeling about what he was reading or writing:

> *He wrote poetry (as if anybody could) before breakfast; he read during breakfast. He wrote history until dinner; he corrected proof sheets between dinner and tea; he wrote an essay for the* Quarterly *afterwards.*

Or his description of the new genre of popular literature well suited to the railway age, so that a traveler could pick up a magazine at a railway stall, peruse it en route, and dispose of it at the end of the line: "People take their literature in morsels, as they take sandwiches in a journey."

If these epigrams are so often double-edged, it is because this duality was, for Bagehot, at the heart of reality. Double-edged – and sharp-edged as well, for his readers were not so much amused as challenged by ideas and sentiments that violated the received wisdom. The Victorians are often decried as hypocritical and mealy-mouthed, given to euphemisms to prettify the "facts of life." Bagehot went to the opposite extreme, deliberately putting matters in their harshest terms. He sometimes prefaced his comments by words like "mischievous," "playful," "provocative," as if to disarm criticism. But his intention was serious enough: to focus upon the difficulties and ambiguities, the hard realities, of politics and society.

There is a bravado in his language, as in his views. He could have made his point about the "stupid people" less offensively, especially because he attributed to them a redeeming common sense, indeed, a wisdom that made democracy viable. There is a strong Tocquevillean streak in *The English Constitution*. But Bagehot, although he quoted Tocqueville and recalled a "memorable" (as he said) meeting with the man, either lacked Tocqueville's felicity in propounding his unconventional views or thought that the times required something more blunt, more audacious.

Today, in an era of political correctness, Walter Bagehot is all the more welcome. He was ironic but not cynical, skeptical but not fatalistic. "Between sizes in politics" as in much else, he may be the right size today. Economists have rediscovered Bagehot. Political philosophers and sociologists should as well.

If he was not the greatest Victorian, he was surely a very great Victorian, as instructive and provocative today as he was a century and more ago.

2013

CHAPTER SIX

Churchill's Welfare State – and Ours

———————■ ⅡⅠⅠⅠ ■———————

THE DEBATE OVER Obamacare may remind a student of British history of the debate in Britain over the National Insurance Act of 1911, which was in effect until the initiation of the welfare state after World War II. The protagonists in that debate (like ours, not formally a debate, but implicitly that) were Winston Churchill, and Sidney and Beatrice Webb. Churchill, a rising star in the Liberal Party and a member of Herbert Asquith's cabinet, heartily promoted the act. The Webbs, prominent members of the Fabian Society and vigorous polemicists ("public intellectuals," we would now call them), sharply criticized it.

Fabianism is generally described as a moderate, reformist type of socialism, achieving its ends not by class war and revolution but by persuasion and "permeation." Yet in a sense it was more radical than Marxism because it sought control not so much of the economy or polity as of society itself. It is fitting that the Fabian Society should have been founded, in 1884, as a society, not a party, for its primary focus was the "social organism," and its ultimate purpose the "regeneration of society," the "reconstruction of the Social System." (If we now speak of the Fabian Society in the past tense, it is because, although it still exists, it has been largely absorbed into the Labour Party.)

Sidney Webb was not literally a founding father of Fabianism, but he was very nearly that. A twenty-six-year-old civil-service clerk (admitted to the bar but not practicing law), he joined the society a year after its establishment and quickly became one of its leading figures. His marriage in 1892 to the no less talented and energetic Beatrice made the couple something like the First Family of Fabianism.

Sidney Webb's contribution to *Fabian Essays in Socialism* (published in 1889 and selling over twenty-five thousand copies in two years) followed the lead essay by the editor, George Bernard Shaw. Where Shaw focused on private property, "the economic action of Individualism," as the nemesis of socialists, Webb made individualism itself the archenemy. Just as the "anarchy" of laissez-faire must be corrected, he argued, so must the "anarchy" in society. The "social organism," once a union of individual men, has evolved, so that the individual is now "created" by the social organism of which he is a part. It is the social organism, therefore, not the individual, that must be cultivated and perfected.

> *The perfect fitting development of each individual is not necessarily the utmost and highest cultivation of his own personality, but the filling, in the best possible way, of his humble function in the great social machine. We must abandon the self-conceit of imagining that we are independent units, and bend our jealous minds, absorbed in their own cultivation, to this subjection to the higher end, the Common Weal.*

Beatrice carried the argument further by extending the case against individualism to a case against democracy as well. In her diary she compared herself and Sidney with her brother-in-law Leonard Courtney, a Liberal member of Parliament and a "democrat at heart."

> *Possibly he is more of a democrat than we are ourselves;*
> *for we have little faith in the "average sensual man," we*
> *do not believe that he can do much more than describe his*
> *grievances, we do not think that he can prescribe the rem-*
> *edies.... We wish to introduce into politics the profes-*
> *sional expert – to extend the sphere of government by*
> *adding to its enormous advantages of wholesale and com-*
> *pulsory management, the advantage of the most skilled*
> *entrepreneur.*

The combination of little faith in the "average sensual man" and complete faith in the "professional expert" was the earmark of Fabianism. "Nothing in England is done," Sidney wrote soon after joining the society, "without the consent of a small intellectual yet practical class in London not 2000 in number.... We, like the homeopathists and the old Radicals, shall win without being acknowledged victors, by permeation of the others." He might have enlarged that figure in later years as the society grew in numbers and influence, but he would have been confirmed in the strategy of "permeation." Sidney dominated the London County Council for many years, Beatrice was an influential member of the Royal Commission on the Poor Laws, and they coauthored the Minority Report in 1909 proposing, among other things, penal colonies for those who refused to work. When they were not permeating the existing institutions of society, they created new ones – the London School of Economics in 1895 and the *New Statesman* magazine in 1913 – all while incessantly writing (more than half a dozen books before the war), lecturing, organizing meetings, and hosting dinner parties that were long on talk and notoriously short on food. (Later Sidney permeated, so to speak, Parliament itself, sitting in the House of Commons for much of the 1920s, until moving to the House of Lords as 1st Baron Passfield.)

———

It may have been the intention of the Webbs to recruit, if not to the Fabian Society, then to their select "class" of experts, a new and promising member of Parliament, Winston Churchill, when they invited him to dinner in 1903. Beatrice's account of him in her diary was hardly favorable, yet not entirely hopeless.

> *First impression; restless – almost intolerably so, without capacity for sustained and unexciting labor – egotistical, bumptious, shallow-minded and reactionary, but with a certain personal magnetism, great pluck and some originality – not of intellect but of character.... No notion of scientific research, philosophy, literature or art, still less religion. But his pluck, courage, resourcefulness and great tradition may carry him far unless he knocks himself to pieces like his father.*

Churchill had then been in Parliament for three years, as a Conservative (like his father), hence Beatrice's characterization of him as "reactionary." But he was something of a maverick from the beginning, which is perhaps why she found him interesting. He was at odds with his party (and his own constituency) principally on the issue of free trade, for social as much as economic reasons. Protectionism, he said, meant "dear food for the million, cheap labor for the millionaire"; workers were justified in seeing tariffs as "taxing every mouthful they eat." But there was something else that must have endeared him to the Webbs. "Our movement," he told a group of Liberals in May 1904, "is towards a better, fairer organization of society" – "organization of society," practically a Fabian slogan. Two weeks later, Churchill moved to the opposition benches, deliberately seating himself next to David Lloyd George – in the same seat his father had occupied during his term in the opposition.

Churchill's rise in the Liberal Party was rapid. One of Henry Campbell-Bannerman's first acts as Liberal prime minister in December 1905 was to appoint Churchill undersecretary of state at the Colonial Office. And one of Herbert Asquith's first acts when he became prime minister in April 1908 was to bring Churchill into the cabinet as president of the Board of Trade. Two years later, Churchill became home secretary and the following year first lord of the Admiralty. By that time, he had supervised and seen through Parliament a series of major reforms: the Old-Age Pensions Act, the Mines Eight-Hours Act, the Labour Exchanges Act, several prison reforms, and the National Insurance Act providing health and unemployment insurance in those industries where unemployment was chronic. The last act was not passed until late in 1911, by which time Churchill was in the Admiralty, but he had been an enthusiastic promoter and defender of it for two years, culminating in the final debate in the House of Commons. To his chagrin, the bill was officially introduced by Lloyd George, the chancellor of the Exchequer. "Lloyd George," Churchill wrote to his wife, "has practically taken Unemployment Insurance to his bosom, and I am I think effectively elbowed out of this large field in which I consumed so much thought and effort. Never mind! There are many good fish in the sea."

Asquith and Lloyd George had been enthusiastic about the bill from the beginning, but the other members of the cabinet were not, which makes Churchill's role all the more important. Unemployment insurance was, as he reminded his wife, the product of "much thought and effort" – and not only unemployment insurance, but social reform in general. "Political freedom, however precious," he wrote in 1908, "is utterly incomplete without a measure at least of social and economic independence." To Asquith, who had visited Germany and been impressed by Bismarck's reforms, he cited that example: "Dimly across gulfs of ignorance I see the outline of a policy which I call the Minimum Standard.... Underneath the immense disjointed fabric of safeguards and insurances which has grown up by itself in England, there must be spread – at a lower level – a sort of Germanised network of State intervention and regulation." Another memorandum, in a curious amalgam of Bismarckianism and Fabianism, proposed a "tremendous policy in Social Organization," including labor exchanges and unemployment and health insurance. "She [Germany] is organized not only for war, but for peace. We are organized for nothing except party politics.... I say – thrust a big slice of Bismarkianism over the whole underside of our industrial system, and await the consequences, whatever they may be, with a good conscience."

If the Webbs would have appreciated Churchill's appeal to "social organization," they did not appreciate the reforms he proposed in that name. Indeed, they were very critical of both the Labour Exchanges Act and the National Insurance Act, for much the same reason: because they were insufficiently rigorous and too permissive, pandering to those they professed to help. The Labour Exchanges Act authorized the Board of Trade to establish "labor exchanges" where workers would be informed of the availability and location of work, be assisted in applying for a job, and be given money to travel to it. The act was voluntary for both the employer and the worker; the employer was not obliged to register his need for labor, nor was the worker obliged to use the facility of the exchange or accept the job offered him.

Introduced by Churchill in 1909 to a nearly empty House of Commons, the Labour Exchanges Act was passed with little dispute. To the Webbs, however, it was deeply flawed. What was wanted, they insisted, was a compulsory system, binding upon employers and laborers alike. Anything short of that would encourage "malingering" on the part of workers, who need not apply to the exchange or accept the job offered them, but could rely on unemployment insurance to support them in lieu of work. "My wife and I," Sidney informed the Board of Trade, "had come to the conclusion that compulsory insurance was impracticable unless we had a compulsory labor exchange; and that, along with a compulsory labor exchange, compulsory insurance was unnecessary." In her diary, Beatrice described her meeting at 11 Downing Street with the lord chancellor followed by a breakfast with Churchill: "I tried to impress on them that any grant from the community to the individual beyond what it does for all, ought to be conditional on better conduct and that any insurance scheme had the fatal defect that the state got nothing for its money – that the persons felt they had a right to the allowance whatever their conduct."

"Conditional on better conduct" – this was at the heart of the issue. The insurance bill was "dangerous" because it provided for "a free choice of doctors," permitting the patient to choose a doctor "who interferes least with his habits" and might order such "medical extras" as food and alcohol. In effect, the bill was "paying the people to be ill." The Webbs recalled the Workmen's Compensation Act of 1897, which tempted workers to make "the most of every mishap," avoid treatment so as to collect compensation, and then squander the money.

It may seem ironic that socialists (of the Fabian or any other variety) should have opposed the National Insurance Act, while a Conservative (temporarily lapsed, to be sure) enthusiastically supported it – and, more ironic, that they both did so under the banner of "social organization." Both took that term seriously, but with different intent. The Webbs wanted to organize society in order to curb the anarchy of individualism and create a rational society in which the average sensual man would be prevented from indulging his whims and vices. Churchill wanted to organize society in order to create the conditions in which individualism would thrive and the average sensual man – that is to say, everyman – could live his life freely, whims, vices, and all. In a memorandum entitled "Notes on Malingering," Churchill defended the proposed act to another Fabian, Llewellyn Smith, the permanent secretary of the Board of Trade:

> *I do not feel convinced that we are entitled to refuse benefit to a qualified man who loses his employment through drunkenness. He has paid his contributions; he has insured himself against the fact of unemployment, and I think it arguable that his foresight should be rewarded irrespective of the cause of his dismissal, whether he lost his situation through his own habits of intemperance or through his employer's habits of intemperance. I do not like mixing up moralities and mathematics.... Our concern*

is with the evil, not with the causes, with the fact of unem-
ployment, not with the character of the unemployed.

"I do not like mixing up moralities and mathematics" – that
memorable sentence encapsulates the debate between
Churchill and the Webbs. The strength and merit of insurance,
Churchill insisted, was that it depended not on the moral, or
immoral, behavior of individuals (of employers and workers
alike, both prone to "habits of intemperance"), but on "clear,
ruthless mathematical rules," the "mathematics of averages."
"We seek to substitute for the pressure of the forces of nature,
operating by chance on individuals, the pressures of the laws
of insurance, operating through averages." He made the same
point in the House of Commons, praising the bill for bringing
"the magic of averages to the aid of the millions."

While repudiating the "moralities" the Webbs brought to
the debate, Churchill attributed to the act a larger moral purpose. By making workers more secure, it would make them
better human beings, and by giving them a "stake in the country"
(in quotation marks), it would also make them better citizens.

The idea is to increase the stability of our institutions by
giving the mass of industrial workers a direct interest in
maintaining them.... With a "stake in the country" in
the form of insurances against evil days the worker will
pay no attention to the vague promises of revolutionary
socialism.... It will help to remove the dangerous ele-
ment of uncertainty from the existence of the industrial
worker. It will give him an assurance that his home, got
together through long years and with affectionate sacri-
fice, will not be broken up, sent bit by bit to the pawnshop,
just because through no fault of his own maybe he falls

out of work. It will make him a better citizen, a more efficient worker, a happier man.

———

This is not the Churchill we remember today, and for good reason. It is a minor episode occupying only a few years in the life of the man who, for more momentous reasons, has been hailed as "the savior of his country," even "the savior of Western civilization." Yet it is a major episode in the social history of his country. And it may be an object lesson for Americans today.

Supporters of Obamacare have praised it as being in the best tradition of progressivism. Critics have decried it as an ominous example of socialism. A more appropriate term might be Fabianism. We may hear the echoes of the Webbs' distrust of the "average sensual man" in the present law that denies the individual a choice of doctors and mandates types of insurance he might not want or require. Or of their reliance upon the "professional expert" to "prescribe the remedies" for the individual's "grievances" in the administrative agencies now authorized to establish the proper medications for all ailments, overriding the doctor as well as the patient. Or of their impatience with the democratic process of legislation in the recent presidential fiats modifying or suspending provisions of the law enacted by Congress. More dramatically, we may see the Fabian vision of the "regeneration of society," the "reconstruction of the Social System," in Barack Obama's exultant pronouncement just before his election: "We are five days away from fundamentally transforming the United States of America."

The National Insurance Act of 1911 may have been a passing event in the life of Churchill. But its American counterpart is a climactic event in the presidency of Barack Obama and a critical event for Americans today. We may well look back to that debate more than a century ago and recall Winston Churchill's quip, upon rejecting an invitation to head the Local Government Board: "I refuse to be shut up in a soup kitchen with Beatrice Webb."

2014

CHAPTER SEVEN

The Jewish Question – Then and Now

—————————————————————

SINCE THE *Charlie Hebdo* affair in January 2015 and the gratuitous, as it seemed, attack on the kosher supermarket in Paris, the condition of Jews in France has been a subject of much discussion and concern, and not only in France. An article in the London *Telegraph* immediately following those murderous events was headlined "Anti-Semitism in France: The Exodus Has Begun."

In fact, both the antisemitism and the exodus had begun earlier, and continue today. An article in the *Washington Post* in May 2016, "Jews Anxious about Future in France," cites the statistics of emigration resulting from a "wave of anti-Semitic violence." This was all the more anxious-making because it was taking place in "the historic fount of liberty, equality and fraternity." A leader of the French Jewish community declared: "Jews – who have been living in France for 2,000 years and have been full citizens since 1791 – now feel that they are looked upon as second-class citizens."

But did Jews live so amicably in France for all of those two thousand years? And was France, for Jews at any rate, the "historic fount of liberty, equality and fraternity" that the French

Enlightenment presumably made her? And did Jews there become "full citizens" even in the first benign years, the pre-Terror years, of the French Revolution? Historians have long been familiar with the antisemitism of the *philosophes*, the mentors of the Enlightenment and the revolution – an antisemitism that was overt and aggressive among some, and more discreet among others.

Voltaire was the most notable and perhaps the least apologetic of the *philosophes*. The great hero of the Enlightenment repeatedly, in his published writings, denounced Jews as barbarous and uncivilized, avaricious and materialistic, and, of course, usurious – although on other occasions he defended the principle of usury against the Catholic Church, which condemned it. More ominous, in the light of subsequent history, was Voltaire's prediction – or threat:

> *I would not be in the least surprised if these people [Jews] would not some day become deadly to the human race.... You [Jews] have surpassed all nations in impertinent fables, in bad conduct, and in barbarism. You deserve to be punished, for this is your destiny.*

"Impertinent fables" was a euphemism for religion, which, for Voltaire as for most of the *philosophes*, was the original sin.

Christianity, and Catholicism in particular, may have been the immediate target of "*Écrasez l'infâme.*" But Judaism was still more infamous as the progenitor of Christianity and of religion in general – hence the primary enemy of "reason," the Enlightenment's guiding principle. If Rousseau and Montesquieu were honorable exceptions to the prevailing antisemitism (the latter even qualifying as philosemitic), it was because they were not committed so absolutely to that principle, and thus were less hostile to religion in general and Judaism in particular. The missing but dominant element in that liturgy of "liberty, equality and fraternity" was reason, which, because of its animus against religion, could, on critical occasions, override the other principles.

As the heir of the Enlightenment, the French Revolution inherited its principles – and its ambiguities. These are encapsulated in the debate culminating in the enfranchisement of Jews in 1791, the "full citizenship" cited as one of the memorable achievements of the revolution. The first article of the Declaration of the Rights of Man and the Citizen, proclaimed in August 1789, pronounced all men "free and equal in rights"; the sixth declared "all citizens, being equal in the eyes of the law, ... equally eligible to all dignities and to all public positions and occupations." On the face of it, Jews seemed to be emancipated as "men" and enfranchised as "citizens." The catch came in the word "citizens."

Shortly after the declaration, the Constituent Assembly passed decrees distinguishing between "active" and "passive" citizens, only the former having the right to vote and bear arms. In addition to such criteria as age, residence, and taxes, the active citizen also had "to be or have become French." That clause had special pertinence to Jews, raising the question of whether all Jews, or only some, were or had become French, therefore qualifying as active citizens. In January 1790, a debate on the subject was closed by Mirabeau, a leading member of the assembly, who declared the Jew a citizen only if he was more a man, *un homme*, than a Jew. A Jew who was more a Jew than *un homme* could not be a citizen; indeed, anyone who did not want to become *un homme* should be banished from the new society created by the revolution. The assembly concluded with a compromise provision. By a vote of 374 to 280, the rights of active citizenship were granted to the three or four thousand Sephardi Jews, specified as "Portuguese, Spanish and Avignonnais Jews."

When the issue came up again the next year, the question focused on the much larger number of Ashkenazi Jews settled mainly in Alsace-Lorraine, who were more conspicuously Jewish. More religious than the Sephardi, less assimilated, and very much a community, the Ashkenazi were charged with being "a nation within a nation." After a long debate, these thirty thousand Jews were declared citizens – as individuals, only if they gave up membership in a religious community. The Count of Clermont-Tonnerre, the deputy from Paris and the chief supporter of the motion, put the case most explicitly. Those Jews who wanted to be citizens must "disavow their judges" and eliminate their "Jewish corporations." "Jews, as individuals, deserve everything; Jews as a nation nothing. . . . There can only be the individual citizen." This was the "full citizenship" that is now heralded as a landmark event in the history of Judaism and of France: Jews could be citizens, but not as Jews.

———

Thirty years later, after the Revolutionary and Napoleonic wars, the subject reappeared, in another country, another context, and with another cast of characters. Responding to a surge of antisemitism in Germany, the most eminent philosopher of the time came to the defense of the Jews. Having earlier propounded a philosophy that made reason (a very different reason from that of the *philosophes*) entirely compatible with religion, Hegel now, in *Philosophy of Right* (1821), argued for the enfranchisement of Jews as a matter of right. It is as if he had the French decree of 1791 in mind as he now insisted upon their full enfranchisement, as Jews and as men. Even if they were regarded as a "religious sect" or "foreign race," this did not deny the fact that "they are, above all, *men*," and as such each "a person with rights." To exclude them from those rights would be a violation of their humanity, and to exclude them from full citizenship a violation of the state as a political institution.

Two decades later, one of Hegel's former disciples, Bruno Bauer (a left-wing Hegelian, as he is now known), turned against the master, reverting, in effect, to the French Enlightenment's disparaging view of religion in general and Judaism in particular. "The Jewish Question" (*Die Judenfrage*), published as an article in 1842 and a pamphlet the following year, is known today mainly because it inspired a critique under the same title by Marx, his former pupil. But Bauer's essay was provocative enough on its own. Decrying all religion as illusory and pernicious, he declared Judaism to be the most degraded form of religion. Against those who defended Jews on the grounds that they had been oppressed and martyred, Bauer insisted that they had brought that condition upon themselves, provoking their enemies by their stubborn adherence to "their law, their language, their whole way of life." While warring against Christianity, they had the audacity to claim citizenship on a par with Christians, asking the Christian state to abandon its religious principles while holding firmly to their own. Since religion itself was a denial of citizenship, Jews could not claim citizenship unless they ceased being Jews.

Marx's critique of Bauer the following year gave a new twist to the "Jewish question." Bauer was being insufficiently radical in assuming that Jews could be enfranchised if they freed themselves of their religion; religious emancipation fell short of "human emancipation." Bauer had considered only the "sabbath Jew." The real problem was the "actual, secular Jew," the "everyday Jew," the Jew whose "worldly cult" was "bargaining" and whose "worldly god" was "money." This was the "practical and real Judaism" from which not only Jews but society itself had to be emancipated. "The social emancipation of the Jew," Marx concluded, "is the emancipation of society from Judaism."

This was the dramatic finale to Marx's "Jewish Question." Jews were twice-damned, as Jews and as capitalists ("usurers," as the stereotype had it). In retrospect, however, Bauer's is really the more radical version, making Jewish identity – a religious, not merely social, identity – the primal source of antisemitism. It is his "Jewish Question" that underlies the equivocal status of Jews in France half a century earlier, as well as the perilous condition of Jews in France today.

———

If Americans can take any comfort in this dispiriting historical retrospect, it is in the thought of how exceptional (as we now say) American history has been – among other things, how different the American Enlightenment and Revolution were from those of the French. Far from seeing reason as antithetical to religion, American thinkers and statesmen, before and after the Revolutionary War, believed reason to be entirely compatible with religion, and religion an integral part of society. Eight years before Bauer's "Jewish Question" appeared, Tocqueville refuted it, at least in regard to America. What had struck him in the United States, he wrote, was how it disproved the *philosophes'* belief that "religious zeal ... will be extinguished as freedom and enlightenment increase." In France, "I had seen the spirit of religion and the spirit of freedom almost always move in contrary directions. Here I found them united intimately with one another; they reigned together on the same soil." The country where Christianity was most influential was also "the most enlightened and free."

Tocqueville's penetrating analysis of the relationship between religion and freedom in France, in contrast to that in the United States, applies as acutely to the situation Jews have encountered in both countries, and, indeed, in much of the world. In this respect, Tocqueville may be said to have the final word on "the Jewish question," as he did on so many others.

2016

Visionaries and Provocateurs

CHAPTER EIGHT

Carlyle: Moralist and Immoralist

I N 1940, Lionel Trilling wrote an essay on T. S. Eliot's *The Idea of a Christian Society*, calling upon his liberal and Marxist friends to be more appreciative of a mode of "religious politics" that was familiar in Victorian times but had come to be regarded as reactionary. "When he [Eliot] says that he is a moralist in politics," Trilling explained, "he means most importantly that politics is to be judged by what it does for the moral perfection, rather than for the physical easement, of man." Trilling's essay, "Elements That Are Wanted," took its title from that Victorian eminence Matthew Arnold, who had said that the function of criticism is "to study and praise elements that for the fulness of spiritual perfection are wanted, even though they belong to a power which in the practical sphere may be maleficent."

It is in this spirit that we should read Thomas Carlyle today, prepared to study and praise him for those elements that "for the fulness of spiritual perfection are wanted," yet in full recognition of their possibly "maleficent" effects when put in practice. And it is in this spirit that his contemporaries read him. We tend to think of the Victorians as conformist, complacent, self-serving. Yet the most eminent of them were highly individualistic, even eccentric, self-questioning, and remarkably self-critical. Thus the most conventional and liberal of them could appreciate, even revere, so iconoclastic and reactionary a thinker as Carlyle.

Thomas Carlyle is a biographer's dream. His life was uneventful in the usual sense; he never had a regular job, or held office, or engaged in any notable activity apart from writing. Yet by sheer force of character he conveys a sense of drama that few public figures could match. The biographer has ample materials to draw on in his personal life: his marriage (probably unconsummated); his tormented relationship with Jane, his intelligent, quick-witted, sharp-tongued wife (the one much-publicized episode of violence, leaving her with bruised wrists, was less traumatic than years of emotional neglect); his lifelong devotion (platonic, but nearly obsessive) to Lady Ashburton, causing much misery to Jane (although not, apparently, to Lord Ashburton); the constant complaints about household problems, servants, noises (a crowing rooster or piano-playing neighbor), each of which took on the proportions of a major crisis; the chronic ailments (with their evocative Victorian names – dyspepsia, colic, biliousness, bowel troubles, lumbago), which somehow did not interfere with travels abroad, visits to family in Scotland and friends in the country; a regimen of exercise that included twenty-mile walks and many hours on horseback; and an aversion to socializing, in spite of which he managed to see a multitude of friends and to meet almost everyone of any importance in England and visitors from abroad.

All the while it was "scribble, scribble, scribble," as was memorably said of Gibbon. And, like Gibbon's, Carlyle's scribbling involved strenuous research. The three volumes on the French Revolution (the first of which had to be rewritten after the manuscript was accidentally burned by John Stuart Mill's housemaid), four on Oliver Cromwell, and six on Frederick the Great may not measure up to modern scholarly standards, but they did represent, for their time, impressive feats of archival research. And they all had respectable sales, in America as well as Britain.

That multivolume works on these subjects, expressing views as unconventional as Carlyle's and in his unique style, should have been so well received is itself remarkable. Only Carlyle could have made heroes of Marie Antoinette, Cromwell, and Frederick, and persuaded the public to give them a sympathetic hearing. But his shorter writings were no less unconventional and were even more enthusiastically received. In many circles Carlyle himself was seen as a hero – or, better yet, a prophet.

Carlyle was thirty-six when his first book appeared in 1831. (He had published several essays earlier.) *Sartor Resartus* might have been expected to kill his career at the outset. If the educated reader of his day understood the meaning of the title ("The Tailor Repatched," for the benefit of the present-day reader), he probably missed most of the German allusions. But he could not have mistaken the laboriously satirical intent of the account of Diogenes *Teufelsdrockh* ("Devilsdung"), professor at the University of *Weissnichtwo* ("Know-not-where"), author of a book on the "Clothes Philosophy," published by *Stillschweigen* ("Silence") & Co. In a style as bizarre as the story itself, the clothes philosophy emerges: All the externalities of civilization are nothing more than the "cloth rags" that conceal the inner reality, the immanent God. Teufelsdrockh himself is said to have come to that reality (as Carlyle did) in the course of a journey from the "Everlasting No" through the "Center of Indifference" to the final revelation of the "Everlasting Yea."

If the God that appears at the end of that journey, a tran-

scendental God stripped of the "Hebrew old clothes" of orthodox Christianity, remains amorphous, there is nothing vague
about the other passions that engage Teufelsdrockh along the
way: his revulsion against materialism, utilitarianism, and
mechanism, against a false democracy that cannot give proper
reverence to leaders and heroes, against the gimmickry of
political reform and the callousness of Malthusianism, and
above all, against the prevalent spirit of Unbelief that denies
not only the spirit of God but the spirit – the soul – of man.

These are the motifs of all of Carlyle's later work, and they
were first presented to an unwary public enveloped in metaphor upon metaphor, in archaisms, solecisms, neologisms,
compound words, and obscure foreign expressions. Publish-
ers were understandably reluctant to take on *Sartor Resartus*,
and eventually it appeared serially in *Fraser's Magazine*, which
promptly lost some subscribers. Yet a modest American edition quickly sold out and a second one was issued, and it was
republished in England a few years later. It won the admiration
not only of Emerson, who wrote a glowing (anonymous) preface to it, but also of John Stuart Mill and George Eliot; it was
read avidly by Matthew Arnold's coterie in Oxford in the
1840s; and it continued to be read, talked about, and reprinted.
In 1900 alone, nine editions were published.

The publication of *Chartism* (1839) ushered in Carlyle's
great decade. It was followed by some of his most influential
works: *Past and Present*; *On Heroes, Hero-Worship, and the
Heroic in History*; and the annotated edition of Cromwell's
letters and speeches (in effect, a biography). Their common
denominator was a radical critique of society – radical not as
most of his contemporaries understood that word, as a call for
liberty and equality, political reforms, and material progress.
What was wanted, Carlyle insisted, was precisely the opposite:

a restoration of authority to bring order out of chaos and give spiritual and social direction to the mass of men. Those exercising this authority must do so by "divine right," which he took to be the opposite of "diabolic wrong." As he wrote in *On Heroes*, "There is no act more moral between men than that of rule and obedience. Woe to him that claims obedience when it is not due; woe to him that refuses it when it is!" Carlyle's critique was directed not against those who mistakenly demanded the "right to rule," but against the ruling classes who had participated in the farce of political reform, thus abdicating their obligation to rule and depriving the people of their true right, the "right to be ruled." In clamoring for the vote, Carlyle said, the Chartists were in fact giving voice to the inarticulate prayer: "Guide me, Govern me! I am mad and miserable, and cannot guide myself."

It is extraordinary that such sentiments were welcomed by those who had acclaimed the reform of the franchise only a few years earlier and who were later to favor its extension. Mill declared *Chartism* "a glorious piece of work" and tried to persuade Carlyle to let him print it in the last issue of the journal he was editing as his valedictory statement.

The year 1850 is generally thought of as the turning point in his life and career, marking the emergence of an even more reactionary Carlyle who was even more dramatically out of tune with his times. It was then that his *Latter-Day Pamphlets* were published, the first of which was the "Occasional Discourse on the Nigger Question." The essay had originally appeared in *Fraser's* as "The Negro Question"; Carlyle changed the title to be more provocative. He had always opposed the antislavery movement on the grounds that it distracted attention from the condition of the working classes at home. The repeal of the Corn Laws, he argued, was more important than the abolition of slavery in the colonies. But in this essay, written long after slavery had been abolished, his diatribe against the "rosepink sentimentalism" of "nigger philanthropists" was calculated to give maximum offense.

Carlyle insisted that he was not defending slavery, which he pronounced a "contradiction of the laws of the universe." The issue, as he saw it, was much larger than that. It was the soul-destroying "dismal science" of political economy, which "finds the secret of this universe in 'supply and demand,' and reduces the duty of human governors to that of letting men alone." What all people required – slaves, serfs, and workers alike – was the right to work and the right to be ruled. And no act of Parliament could provide them with these elementary rights.

There was little in this essay that was not in Carlyle's earlier writings. But it was put so harshly here that Mill was moved to write a sharp (although anonymous) reply in *Fraser's*, which effectively broke off their friendship. Carlyle's response was to go on the offensive against other liberal "sentimentalisms," as he saw them. In subsequent pamphlets, he criticized the movement against capital punishment and satirized the "model prisons" that treated criminals better than paupers, proposed putting beggars and the unemployed to work in compulsory "regiments," deplored petty statesmen and mocked Parliament as a "talking shop," and reviled not only Catholicism but all organized religions that were prone to "Jesuitism," the sin of cant.

The *Latter-Day Pamphlets* were not as well received by reviewers as the earlier writings. Yet they sold well, as did most of Carlyle's later work, which was no less provocative. His last essay, "Shooting Niagara," written immediately after the Reform

Act of 1867 enfranchised most of the working classes, described an England in a state of social and spiritual anarchy, betrayed by its natural aristocracies: the "speculative" aristocracy (literary and artistic) that was wasting itself on trivia, and the "practical" or "industrial" aristocracy that was mired in the "cheap and nasty." Reprinted as a pamphlet, it sold seven thousand copies within weeks. At the same time, a new edition of his collected works was being issued. By now his writings earned him a substantial income, so that he found, much to his surprise, that he was no longer the impoverished writer he had always thought himself. (He had also received a handsome bequest from Lord Ashburton.)

Far from becoming a pariah as a result of these "infamous" writings, as some later biographers would call them, Carlyle counted among his friends and admirers Emerson, Ruskin, Tennyson, Dickens, Thackeray, Macaulay, Browning, Henry Adams, and a host of others. He was elected to the Athenaeum and, later, to the honorary position of rector of Edinburgh University, succeeding Gladstone. (The unsuccessful candidate was Disraeli.) Turning down other invitations from royalty, he reluctantly agreed to an audience with the queen, taking the occasion, she noted in her journal, to declaim upon "the utter degeneration of everything." He refused the offer of a knighthood from Disraeli (that "superlative Hebrew conjuror"), but accepted a doctorate from Harvard. When he died, in February 1881, the dean of Westminster tried to persuade his niece, who had lived with him, to have him interred in Westminster Abbey with the other eminences of England. But she would not go against his expressed wish, which was to be buried in the small Scottish town where he had been born.

"No man else," Walt Whitman said in his eulogy, "will bequeath to the future more significant hints of our stormy era, its fierce paradoxes, its din, and its struggling parturition periods, than Carlyle." The dean of Westminster, in his sermon in the Abbey, endorsed the title of "prophet" that was often bestowed on Carlyle – a prophet, he said, for an "untoward generation," resisting the modern tendency of "exalting popular opinion and popular movements as oracles to be valued above the judgment of the few, above the judgment of the wise, the strong, and the good." Some of the obituaries, like many later commentaries, faulted Carlyle for being overly critical of the existing institutions of society and insufficiently constructive in proposing alternative ones. But this is to misunderstand the function of the prophet, which is precisely to criticize rather than to construct. Indeed, it can be dangerous, as Trilling intimated, to apply the exhortations of the prophet to the practical sphere, where they may well prove to be "maleficent."

This is why Carlyle, like all prophets, had many admirers but few disciples. The Victorians, or at least the most eminent of them, did not make the mistake of confusing the prophetic mode with the practical. They could appreciate the spiritual force of Carlyle's teachings – his criticisms of the "pig-philosophy" of utilitarianism, the "mammonism" of materialism, the "sans-culottism" of democracy, the "cash-nexus" of laissez-faire, and all the other "soul-murdering Mud-Gods" that governed their lives – while retaining the safe and familiar institutions and practices that were, if not entirely beneficent, at least not maleficent.

The economist and social critic Harriet Martineau, herself a firm advocate of laissez-faire, arranged a lecture series for Carlyle in which he attacked that doctrine, among other things. He was an "original," she explained, a messenger come with tidings from "the Infinite Unknown," the "primal reality of things." After the publication of his most provocative pamphlets, George Eliot paid tribute to him: "There is hardly a superior or active mind of his generation that has not been modified by Carlyle's writings; there has hardly been an English book written for the last ten or twelve years that would not have been different if Carlyle had not lived."

Carlyle was the conscience of an age that was conscience-ridden and guilt-stricken, not only about its vices but about its virtues as well. Matthew Arnold confided to a friend:

> *These are damned times – everything is against one – the height to which knowledge is come, the spread of luxury, our physical enervation, the absence of great natures, the unavoidable contact with millions of small ones, newspapers, cities, light profligate friends, moral desperadoes like Carlyle, our own selves, and the sickening consciousness of our difficulties.*

But then, he continued, as if to caution against such moral desperadoes: "For God's sake let us neither be fanatics nor yet chaff blown by the wind but let us be 'virtuous as the man of practical wisdom would define it.'" (The quotation from Aristotle was, of course, in Greek in Arnold's letter.)

A hostile commentator might interpret this kind of self-criticism as moral posturing, a typical bit of Victorian hypocrisy. Not Simon Heffer, whose biography of Carlyle owes its title to Arnold. *Moral Desperado* takes seriously the moral as well as the desperate nature of his hero. This is both the merit of the book and its inevitable shortcoming. If Carlyle is, in his life and mind, a biographer's delight – passionate, contentious, melodramatic – he is also a biographer's despair. How does one convey, in the cold, rational format of the conventional biography, proceeding in an orderly fashion from month to month, year to year, the inner turmoil that is rarely reflected in external events? And how does one avoid the discordance between commentary and quotation – between the lucid prose of the biographer and the eccentric, chaotic, often manic style in which Carlyle's ideas were embodied, and which was so appropriate to those ideas? Henry James, himself not the most crystalline of writers, said of Carlyle's style that "it is not defensible but it is victorious."

Yet for all of that, any serious biography of Carlyle, like Heffer's, is to be welcomed. For if we have good reason to reject his reactionary ideas – about slavery, most notably – we may be appreciative of his critique of some of the prevailing liberal ideas. Carlyle is assuredly not our prophet. But he does remind us of the need for prophets who will keep in the forefront of our imagination those "elements that for the fulness of spiritual perfection are wanted."

1997

CHAPTER NINE

Disraeli: Der Alte Jude

A RECENT BOOK published by the Yale University Press, a biography of the nineteenth-century British prime minister Benjamin Disraeli, opens provocatively: "Does Benjamin Disraeli deserve a place in a series of books called Jewish Lives?" Perhaps not, a reader of the book might well conclude. Disraeli has always been a challenge, to Jews and non-Jews, contemporaries as well as biographers. But rereading the man himself, I was reassured that he is entirely worthy of a place in "Jewish Lives" (and justified the considerable space I gave him a few years ago in *The People of the Book*).

Though formally Anglican – his father had him baptized when he was twelve, before the rite of bar mitzvah – Disraeli identified himself, and was generally identified, as a Jew. He bore a conspicuously Jewish name, changing his father's D'Israeli only by removing the apostrophe. He made no secret of his heritage in his speeches and writings, and he flaunted it in his person, deliberately cultivating a Jewish appearance. His novels dramatized a politics imbued with Judaism and a "new Crusade" that would restore Christianity to its Jewish origins. All of this in mid-Victorian England, when Jews were the villains of novels and the butt of satirists, when they could not even have a seat in Parliament, much less climb to "the top of the greasy pole," as Disraeli put it. (Not one has climbed it after him; there has been no Jewish prime minister since his death in 1881.)

While climbing that pole, Disraeli wrote no fewer than fifteen novels, his first in 1826 at the age of twenty-one and his last in 1880, with another, unfinished one published posthumously. His father, Isaac D'Israeli, a writer, scholar, and man-about-town (who never converted), once cautioned his son: "How will the Fictionist assort with the Politician?" But assort they did. In 1833, in a private journal, Disraeli implicitly responded to the familiar charge that the novels were frivolous, unrealistic fantasies. *Vivian Grey*, he said, "portrayed my active and real ambition"; *The Wondrous Tale of Alroy* "my ideal ambition"; *Contarini Fleming* "my poetic character." The trilogy was "the secret history of my feelings."

If those early novels, which predated his political career, reveal his private life, another trilogy, written in the mid-1840s when he was firmly established in Parliament, are as revelatory of his public persona. *Coningsby* (1844), in effect his political testament, was an attack on the "Tweedledum and Tweedledee" characters (the followers of Prime Minister Robert Peel) who were reducing the Conservatives to a party of "Tory men and Whig measures," and a defense of the "new generation" of the subtitle (the Young Englanders, led by Disraeli), who sought to preserve the venerable institutions of Crown and Church. *Sybil*, his social testament published the following year, was a commentary on the "two nations" of the subtitle, the ominous class divide between the poor and the rich, which could only be overcome by policies favoring the poor and re-creating the "one nation" of the old Tories.

Tancred, which completed the trilogy in 1847, was his spiritual and, one might say, Judaic testament. It is not surprising to find premonitions of *Tancred* in *Coningsby*, in which the "new generation" was called upon to restore the historic relationship of church and state. Two years later, in the preface to a new edition of *Coningsby*, Disraeli looked to the church itself for the "renovation of the national spirit." This, in turn, moved him to "ascend to the origin of the Christian Church" – to the "race which had founded Christianity."

> *The Jews were looked upon in the middle ages as an accursed race, the enemies of God and man, the especial foes of Christianity. No one in those days paused to reflect that Christianity was founded by the Jews; that its Divine Author, in his human capacity, was a descendant of King David; that his doctrines avowedly were the completion, not the change, of Judaism.... The time had arrived when some attempt should be made to do justice to the race which had founded Christianity.*

That "race" appeared in *Coningsby* in the person of Sidonia, the stranger who inspired the title character to undertake the difficult task of spiritual "renovation." Sidonia, like Coningsby, is an aristocrat, but of a different order, a scion of that "unmixed race," "the aristocracy of Nature." Descended from the *cristianos nuevos*, the Marranos of Spain and Portugal who secretly observed Jewish laws and rites, Sidonia had emigrated to England, where he could openly profess his faith. It is there he met Coningsby, infecting him with the ideals that would transform English politics.

Sidonia reappears in *Tancred*, where he delivers the message: "All is race; there is no other truth." Tancred (Lord Montacute) is also an aristocrat, the only son of the Duke of Bellamont.

Like Coningsby, he too is at odds with the political establishment. Repelled by the materialism and soullessness of his class, he refuses to enter Parliament, informing his father that he wants instead to make a pilgrimage to the "Holy Land," the "sepulchre of my Saviour." He hopes there to discover "what is Duty, and what is Faith? What ought I to Do and what ought I to Believe?" At the suggestion of a friend, Tancred calls upon Sidonia, the Jewish banker, for advice: "I am born in an age and in a country divided between infidelity on one side and an anarchy of creeds on the other; with none competent to guide me, yet feeling that I must believe, for I hold that duty cannot exist without faith." Was it unreasonable, he asks, to do what his ancestors would have done six centuries earlier? "It appears to me, Lord Montacute," Sidonia replies, "that what you want is to penetrate the great Asian mystery." It is that mission, the "new Crusade" of the subtitle, that Tancred enthusiastically undertakes.

From London to Jerusalem – it is another world and another time that Tancred enters. Disraeli himself had made that voyage in 1831, ending up among "that sacred and romantic people from whom I derive by blood and name." Now, in the person of Tancred, he repeats it. Walking from the garden of Gethsemane toward Bethany, he sees in its colorful past evidence of "a living, a yet breathing and existing city." He also meets the woman who personifies that spirit. Fatigued by his walk, he falls asleep and awakens to find a young woman standing before him, richly garbed and bejeweled, her face "the perfection of oriental beauty." Their conversation quickly establishes the fact that he is Christian and she Jewish. Exploring the similarities and differences of their faiths, the woman concludes that they have one thing in common. "We agree that half Christendom worships a Jewess, and the other half a

Jew. . . . Which do you think should be the superior race, the worshipped or the worshippers?" Tancred is about to answer, but she has vanished. She is later identified as Eva Besso, the "Rose of Sharon," the daughter of the Jewish banker to whom Sidonia had written a letter of introduction for Tancred.

Much of the rest of the book is an adventure tale in an exotic setting. The adventures are brought about by Eva's foster brother, Fakredeen, a clever and unscrupulous Syrian who is plotting to bring all of Palestine under his control. As a result of his intrigues, Tancred is taken prisoner, wounded, and finally released, all the while engaging with his captor in animated discourses about their respective faiths. At one point, Tancred confesses to himself the failure of his mission. His presence in the Holy Land, he had thought, would bring him into communion with the Holy Spirit. But in spite of his prayers, he has received no such sign, suggesting the desolate thought "that there is a qualification of blood as well as of locality necessary for this communion, and that the favored votary must not only kneel in the Holy Land but be of the holy race." Was he an unwelcome visitor to this land, he wonders? Was it only morbid curiosity or aristocratic restlessness that had brought him here? He tries to reassure himself that he is not like the Indian Brahmin touring a foreign country. It is as an Englishman that he feels a natural and intimate relation to the Holy Land.

> *Vast as the obligations of the whole human family are to the Hebrew race, there is no portion of the modern populations so much indebted to them as the British people. . . . We are indebted to the Hebrew people for our knowledge of the true God and for the redemption from our sins. . . . I come to the land whose laws I obey, whose religion I profess, and I*

seek, upon its sacred soil, those sanctions which for ages were abundantly accorded.

In the final scene of the book, in the garden of Bethany where they first met, Eva confirms his doubts. He had come, she tells him, seeking a "divine cause," looking for "stars" and "angels" in this "peculiar and gifted land." But it is now all mixed up with intrigue, schemes, and politics. "You may be, you are, free from all this, but your faith is not the same. You no longer believe in Arabia" (the contemporary term for Palestine). "Why, thou to me art Arabia," he insists. "Talk not to me of leaving a divine cause; why, thou art my cause, and thou art most divine." She persists: "There are those to whom I belong, and to whom you belong. . . . Fly, fly from me, son of Europe and of Christ!" Why should he fly? he protests. He is a Christian in the land of Christ. He will not leave until she agrees that "our united destinies shall advance the sovereign purpose of our lives." If only she declares her love for him, he will sever the "world-worn bonds" that constrain them. That she cannot do. Her head falls upon his shoulder, he embraces her, but her cheek is cold, her hand lifeless. He sprinkles her with water from the fountain. She opens her eyes, sighs, and looks about her in bewilderment. At that moment, noises are heard. People come trampling toward them, with shouts for Lord Montacute. The party appears. "The Duke and Duchess of Bellamont had arrived at Jerusalem."

That last sentence of the book comes as a shock to the reader. What are Tancred's parents doing in Jerusalem, and what does their arrival signify for him and for his divine but perhaps lost cause? Does it mean that the established order is reasserting itself, fettering Tancred again with those "world-

worn bonds"? Or have the duke and duchess, the most eminent of Englishmen, come to sympathize with his crusade,
even accredit his cause? Some critics find this ambiguity a fatal
flaw in the book. Disraeli himself never had second thoughts
about it or its message. Thirty years later, as prime minister
much involved with the "Eastern question" (a variant of the
"Arabian" one), he told his friend Benjamin Jowett, the master
of Balliol, that *Tancred* was his favorite of his novels.

———

"How will the Fictionist assort with the Politician?" his father
had asked him. Very well, the son could have assured him. Six
months after the publication of *Tancred*, Disraeli delivered a
speech in Parliament echoing the novel – indeed, going even
further in drawing out its political implications. Where William Gladstone and others argued in favor of the Jewish Dis-
abilities Bill on the grounds of religious liberty, and others
opposed it because that liberty violated the established religion, Disraeli insisted that it was precisely for religious reasons
that Jews should be admitted to Parliament. "There is something more excellent than religious liberty – and that more
excellent thing is religious truth." And not only religious truth,
but "religious truth taking the shape of religious conformity" –
that is, a religion consonant with the established church.

> *Who are these persons professing the Jewish religion? They
> are persons who acknowledge the same God as the Chris-
> tian people of this realm. They acknowledge the same
> divine revelation as yourselves. They are, humanly speak-
> ing, the authors of your religion. They are unquestionably*

those to whom you are indebted for no inconsiderable por-
tion of your known religion, and for the whole of your
divine knowledge.

Interrupted by cries of outrage, Disraeli went on to defend his position on moral as well as religious grounds. Surely, he argued, to those who "profess the religion which every gentle-man in this House professes – for every gentleman here does profess the Jewish religion, and believes in Moses and the Prophets ... [well], then I say that if religion is a security for righteous conduct, you have that security in the instance of the Jews who profess a true religion." However degraded a Jew might have become as a result of centuries of persecution, he was "sustained by the divine law he obeys, and by the sublime morality he professes." It is as Christians, therefore, and in a Christian assembly, that Parliament should welcome the Jews – those "who are of the religion in the bosom of which my Lord and Savior was born."

Four years after that speech in the Commons, Disraeli took the occasion to repeat that theme in an unlikely context. In the midst of his biography of the recently deceased George Bentinck, his friend and Tory ally, he gratuitously inserted a chapter entitled "The Jewish Question" – gratuitously, because Bentinck's name does not even appear in that chapter, and his only connection with Judaism was his support of the Jewish emancipation bills (on the very grounds of liberty that Disraeli had dismissed). The chapter is nothing less than a paean to "the Jewish race," a race "sustained by a sublime religion," which had survived the hatred and persecution of centuries. Surveying the accomplishments of Jews in every sphere of life, he concluded that "no existing race is so much entitled to the esteem and gratitude of society as the Hebrew." Far from being guilty of the crucifixion, they could proudly claim Jesus, "born from the chosen house of the chosen people," as one of them.

It was an odd and passionate digression in an otherwise prosaic biography of a politician (and non-Jew), all the more conspicuous because Disraeli had nothing to gain from it – indeed, everything to lose by it. He was at a point in his career when he had to present himself to his Tory constituency as a "sound man," and there was already much about him that seemed to be unsound, in his name and person, his politics and novels. *Tancred* could be read as a fantasy, a *jeu d'esprit* – or "Jew *d'esprit*," as was said. But his tributes to Jews and Judaism, in and out of Parliament, could not be so easily dismissed.

———

Decades later, in his second term as prime minister, Disraeli confronted one of the main crises of his career – not the "Jewish question" but the "Eastern question." The growing aggressiveness of Russia and her victory in her war with Turkey, giving her control over the Dardanelles and the Mediterranean, were of obvious concern to Britain and the rest of Europe. Against members of his own party, including the foreign secretary, who, as Disraeli told the queen, was "for doing nothing," Disraeli took an even more aggressive tone, abroad and at home. In 1878 at the Congress of Berlin, he emerged as the dominant figure and combatant. By being bold and persistent, threatening to break up the congress and even declare war on Russia, he succeeded in reversing Russia's gains and resolving the crisis in favor of Britain and Europe.

Disraeli returned home in triumph, to the plaudits of the queen and much of the nation. But perhaps his greatest tribute came not from an Englishman or a Jew but from the prime minister of Prussia. It was affectionately and admiringly – not cynically or derisively, as one might suspect – that Otto von Bismarck hailed him: "*Der alte Jude, das ist der Mann.*" Almost forty years later, Winston Churchill, whose own praise of "the Jewish race" almost rivals Disraeli's, recalled "the Jew Prime Minister of England," who, "true to his race and proud of his origin," said on one memorable occasion: "The Lord deals with the nations as the nations deal with the Jews."

Yes, "the old Jew," "the Jew Prime Minister," deserves an honorary, indeed, honorable place among "Jewish Lives" and "The People of the Book."

2016

CHAPTER TEN

Cardinal Newman:
Education and Christianity

——————■ ■ ■ ■ ■ ■————————

IT WILL BE some time before Yale University recovers from the Bass fiasco – the refusal to abide by an agreement with Lee Bass in the early 1990s that would have generously funded a program in Western civilization. In the meantime, Yale University Press is doing its bit by way of atonement in reprinting some of the classics of Western civilization in a series entitled "Rethinking the Western Tradition." The "rethinking" refers to essays from contributors representing different points of view, but even the most critical of these commentaries cannot detract from the works themselves. The first two volumes are Matthew Arnold's *Culture and Anarchy*, edited by Samuel Lipman, and *The Idea of a University* by John Henry Newman, edited by Frank M. Turner. Both are impeccably edited, with challenging commentaries and enough scholarly apparatus to satisfy an academic audience without intimidating the lay reader. And both are even more pertinent today than when they were published.

The Idea of a University consists of a series of lectures delivered by Newman in 1852, supplemented by a few in the following years, which were meant to establish the principles of the new Catholic University in Dublin, of which he was the first rector. It was a curious situation: Newman, a recent convert to Catholicism, trying to persuade Irish Catholics to support a university modeled on Oxford (which did not admit Catholics) and a "liberal education" that included theology as part of the curriculum. Theology was what Newman insisted upon – not religious piety, as many Catholics understood it, still less religious sentiment or feeling, as some Protestants thought of it, but theology as an "intellectual act, its object truth, and its result knowledge." Theology in this sense was as much a part of "universal knowledge" as science or philosophy. There was no conflict between science and theology, any more than there was between "nature and grace, reason and revelation," because all came from "the same Divine Author, whose works cannot contradict each other."

If many Catholics were not persuaded by the idea of a liberal education, they were hardly reassured by Newman's observation that such an education was designed to produce "not the Christian, not the Catholic, but the gentleman." And not the manners and habits of the gentleman, which could be acquired by good society, foreign travel, and the "innate grace of the Catholic." The particular characteristics of the gentleman that came from a liberal education were "a cultivated intellect, a delicate taste, a candid, equitable, dispassionate mind, a noble and courteous bearing in the conduct of life."

It was almost as if Newman was determined to offend all of his natural allies. If the idea of a liberal, gentlemanly education sounded suspiciously secular, even Protestant, to most Catholics, liberals were put off by the idea of theology as part of the curriculum. And the academic establishment in general was disturbed by the principle enunciated in the opening sentences of the very first lecture: that the university should be "a place of *teaching* universal *knowledge*." The italics were in the original, emphasizing Newman's insistence upon teaching rather than research – the "diffusion and extension" of knowledge rather than its "advancement" by way of new discoveries. If research and discovery were the purpose of a university, he asked, why have students at all? Why not create academies on the French model, or associations and societies, like the British Association or the Royal Society? Moreover, the knowledge cultivated at the university was knowledge as its own end, for its own sake. Useful and professional knowledge (medicine or the law) had its place, but not in a university.

In one respect, Newman was in accord with the prevalent opinion of his day. A liberal education was an education in "civilization," the civilization that began, he specified, in Palestine and Greece and became Christian civilization as we now know it. The "outlying portions of mankind" – "Chinese, or Hindoo, or Mexican, or Saracenic" – were just that, not part of "the representative Society and Civilization of the human race." It is this view of civilization that has given the Greek classics a preeminent part in the university, for they have been the instruments of education that "the civilized *orbis terrarium*" has adopted.

There is enough here to challenge and provoke the contributors to this volume. If Newman often seems to go out of his way to quarrel with his own contemporaries, he also anticipates some of the most important disputes engaging academics today. Thus the editor finds Newman's idea of a liberal education a valuable corrective to the "provincialisms" of ethnicity, gender, and sexual orientation that dominate the university today, while another contributor is troubled by Newman's hostility to new knowledge and ways of thinking, by his commitment to a civilization that logically leads to imperialism, segregation, and apartheid, and by his idea of a universal knowledge that obscures the realities of cultural politics. Our current debates about multiculturalism and Eurocentrism, religion and morality, professionalism and specialization, teaching and research, the canon and the curriculum – all of these leap out of Newman's pages to the reader today.

Even computers and cybernetics become an issue, as we read Newman rejecting in advance, as it were, the suggestion of one contributor that the next stage in the information revolution is an electronic university, with virtual texts existing only in cyberspace. We recall Newman asking which was the better university: one that dispensed with residence and tutorial superintendence and gave its degrees on the basis of examinations alone, or one that had no professors or exams but brought young men together for three years, as Oxford in its worst days did? He had no hesitation, he said, in favoring the latter, for the school itself was a *genius loci*, a requirement of our "social being," providing for the development of character, the discipline of the intellect, and the enlargement of the mind.

Still more pertinent today – and, in some circles, more controversial – are Newman's remarks on the university as the "umpire between truth and truth," respecting the boundaries of each province of knowledge, taking into account the nature and importance of each, and assigning to all their "due order of precedence." Truth: this was what Newman's university was all about. In our own universities, this idea has become almost as bizarre as the idea of the student or professor as a gentleman, or gentlewoman.

1996

CHAPTER ELEVEN

T. H. Huxley:
Evolution and Ethics

————————■ ⅠⅠⅠⅠⅠ ■————————

"THEY PERSUADE THE WORLD of what is false by urging upon it what is true." That is John Henry Newman in *The Idea of a University* (1852) referring to the sciences of his day, which threatened to dominate and even overwhelm theological education in the university. A science's teaching might be true in its proper place but fallacious "if it be constituted the sole exponent of all things in heaven and earth, and that, for the simple reason that it is encroaching on territory not its own, and undertaking problems which it has no instruments to solve."

While Newman's notion of science was far broader than ours, including even painting and music, his description of the over-reach of science is still apt. We now have a term for that fallacy, "scientism," exemplified by Richard Dawkins's pronouncement that genes "created us, body and mind," and by Edward O. Wilson's claims for "the biological basis of all social behavior." That scientism has become so prevalent is partly because of the emergence of new sciences, each encroaching, as Newman said, on "territory not its own" (invading the turf of others, we would now say), and each professing to comprehend – in both senses of that word – the whole. Intended as an epithet, the term has been adopted as an honorific by some of its practitioners. A chapter in the book *Every Thing Must Go: Metaphysics Naturalized* (2007) by three philosophers is entitled "In Defense of Scientism."

Newman's book appeared seven years before Charles Darwin's *On the Origin of Species*, which provoked the classic case of scientism: the mutation of Darwinism into social Darwinism. There had been earlier theories of evolution, such as Lamarck's. And there had been earlier doctrines, most notably Malthus's, that applied to society the concept of a "struggle for existence." Indeed, Darwin had been inspired by Malthus, while opposing Lamarck. But it was the *Origin of Species* that gave credibility to the theory of evolution and, inadvertently, encouraged others to extend it to society, making the "survival of the fittest" the natural and proper basis for human behavior and social relations.

The emergence of social Darwinism recalls the adage of another eminent Victorian. "Ideas," wrote Lord Acton, "have a radiation and development, an ancestry and posterity of their own, in which men play the part of godfathers and godmothers more than that of legitimate parents." Darwin, the unwitting godfather of social Darwinism, disowned even that degree of parentage. He dismissed as ludicrous the charge of one reviewer that he had endorsed "might is right," thereby justifying the idea "that Napoleon is right & every cheating Tradesman is also right." Challenged on another occasion to declare his views on religion, he replied that while the subject of God was "beyond the scope of man's intellect," his moral obligation was clear: "man can do his duty." Averse to controversy in general (even over the *Origin of Species* itself), Darwin played no public part in the dispute over social Darwinism. That battle was left to his "bulldog," as T. H. Huxley proudly described himself; Darwin called him "my general agent." Huxley's arguments against social Darwinism are all the more telling because they come not, as might have been expected, from a cleric or theologian, but from an eminent scientist and ardent Darwinist.

Sixteen years younger than Darwin, with little formal schooling, self-taught and self-willed, Thomas Henry Huxley (like Darwin) served his apprenticeship as a naturalist by doing research on a royal naval ship (although his official appointment was as assistant surgeon). By the time he returned from that four-year trip, he was a recognized authority on marine biology. In 1851, at the age of twenty-six, he was elected a Fellow of the Royal Society; the following year he received the Royal Medal; and two years later he was appointed Professor of Natural History at the Royal School of Mines. It was around this time, while Darwin was laboring on early drafts of the *Origin of Species*, that Huxley met him and became one of his three principal confidants and advisers, and by far the youngest. (The others were Charles Lyell and Joseph Hooker.) "If I can convert Huxley," Darwin wrote in November 1859, when the *Origin* was published, "I shall be content." Huxley needed conversion because he had been wary of other theories of evolution and even of Darwin's in its earlier stages. But he was completely won over after reading the book. "My reflection," Huxley recalled, "when I first made myself master of the central idea of the 'Origin' was, 'How extremely stupid not to have thought of that!'" Preparing Darwin for the "abuse and misrepresentation" the book would receive, Huxley reassured him: "I am sharpening up my claws and beak in readiness."

As there had been earlier theories of evolution, so there were earlier versions of social Darwinism, most notably the laissez-faire propounded by Herbert Spencer. It took a while for Huxley to address that issue, perhaps because Spencer was a friend (and remained one, in spite of their differences). But when he did, he brought to its refutation the same vigor he brought to the defense of the *Origin*. Provoked by recent demands to deny the state any role in education, Huxley, in his 1871 lecture "Administrative Nihilism," supported the state in that capacity as in others, arguing that men are not isolated individuals but parts of a "social organization," requiring all the help and support that society can and should give them so that each may attain "all the happiness which he can enjoy without diminishing the happiness of his fellow-men." He expanded upon that theme in his 1888 essay "The Struggle for Existence in Human Society," distinguishing between nature and society, man as an animal and man as a human – which is to say, moral – being:

> *From the point of view of the moralist the animal world is on about the same level as a gladiator's show. The creatures are fairly well treated, and set to fight – whereby the strongest, the swiftest, and the cunningest live to fight another day. . . .*
>
> *Society differs from nature in having a definite moral object; whence it comes about that the course shaped by the ethical man – the member of society or citizen – necessarily runs counter to that which the non-ethical man – the primitive savage, or man as mere member of the animal kingdom – tends to adopt. The latter fights out the struggle for existence to the bitter end, like any other*

animal; the former devotes his best energies to the object of setting limits to the struggle.

———

Five years later, Huxley produced the classic case against social Darwinism – and against scientism in general. "Evolution and Ethics," delivered at Oxford in 1893, was the second of the prestigious Romanes Lectures, the first having been given the year before by the prime minister, William Gladstone. The choice of Gladstone as the initial lecturer was surprising in view of the conditions laid down by the sponsor, George Romanes, that the lecturer, as Huxley explained, "abstain from treating of either Religion or Politics," the two subjects about which Gladstone was most passionate. A skilled rhetorician, Gladstone managed to address his theme, "Medieval Universities," while skirting as best he could any overt mention of religion, even though it was central to his argument. Huxley, too, had to perform an "egg-dance," as he said, reassuring Romanes that there would be no allusion to politics in his lecture and that his only reference to religion was to Buddhism, and this only to the "speculative and ethical side" of it. In fact, politics does appear, if only implicitly. Spencer's name is not mentioned, but he is clearly implicated in Huxley's decrying of the "fanatical individualism of our time." In a footnote to the published version, Huxley adds that "it is this form of political philosophy to which I conceive the epithet of 'reasoned savagery' to be strictly applicable."

Published as an essay the following year, the forty-one-page lecture is prefaced by forty-five pages of "Prolegomena" and supplemented by thirty pages of footnotes, exhibiting a remarkable range and depth of knowledge of philosophy in particular – this not from a philosopher but a scientist (and an autodidact at that). Indeed, philosophy, rather than politics, bears the burden of the argument over social Darwinism. The epigraph from Seneca, in Latin, may be translated: "For I am wont to cross over even into the enemy's camp, – not as a deserter, but as an explorer." This precisely defines Huxley's role. The scientist is venturing into the enemy camp, that of the philosopher and moralist, not as a deserter from science, but as an explorer – and discovering not an enemy, but a welcome ally.

The essay opens, less formidably, with a "delightful child's story," "Jack and the Bean-stalk," the familiar tale of "a bean-plant, which grows and grows until it reaches the high heavens and there spreads out into a vast canopy of foliage." The hero, climbing the stalk, finds that the world of the foliage above is made up of the same parts as the world below, "yet strangely new," for as the stalk grows and expands, it "undergoes a series of metamorphoses," and then, having reached ever new heights, it begins to wither and crumble. This tale of "cyclical evolution" illustrates the "cosmic process" (a term that is almost a refrain in the essay) that governs mankind as well as the animal kingdom, but with a difference. The pain and suffering inherent in that process affects all living creatures, but man more intensely, and civilized man, the member of an "organized polity," more than the savage.

Man, the animal, in fact, has worked his way to the head-ship of the sentient world, and has become the superb animal which he is, in virtue of his success in the struggle for existence.... But, in proportion as men have passed from anarchy to social organization, and in proportion

*as civilization has grown in worth, these deeply ingrained
serviceable qualities have become defects. After the manner of successful persons, civilized man would gladly kick
down the ladder by which he has climbed. He would be
only too pleased to see "the ape and tiger die."*

As savagery gave way to civilization, civilization itself became
problematic. "The stimulation of the senses, the pampering of
the emotions," and the cultivation of the intellectual and imagi-
native faculties led to a weakening of old customs and traditions, including primitive ideas of justice. Only with the further
advance of civilization was justice refined, distinguishing
between voluntary and involuntary misdeeds, doling out punishment in accord with motive, and making justice an instrument of "righteousness" rather than mere revenge. It was at
this stage that civilized man was superseded by "ethical man,"
who, rejecting the "ape and tiger promptings" of nature,
branded them as sins and punished them as crimes. It was
then that philosophers sought to reconcile the implacable facts
of evolution, of nature itself, with "the ethical ideal of the just
and the good."

At this point, Huxley comes close to defying Romanes's
injunction about religion. He does steer clear of Christianity,
to be sure; Jesus, the New Testament, and the Church Fathers
are conspicuously absent from his account. But the Book of
Job and the Buddhist sutras are amply cited to illustrate "the
unfathomable injustice of the nature of things": "that the
wicked flourishes like a green bay tree, while the righteous
begs his bread; that the sins of the fathers are visited upon the

children." While Job took refuge in "silence and submission," Buddhists sought to vindicate the cosmic process with the "doctrine of transmigration," and Indian philosophers invoked the concept of "karma" for the same purpose.

The Greek philosophers took different approaches to the problem. Several of the pre-Socratic philosophers, especially Heraclitus, were "pronounced evolutionists," their aphorisms and metaphors anticipating some of the modern doctrine. Socrates and the Athenians, on the other hand, engaged in "a kind of inverse agnosticism," putting physics "beyond the reach of the human intellect" and enjoining philosophers to devote themselves to the study of ethics, "the one worthy object of investigation." The Stoics, professing to be disciples of Heraclitus, altered his teachings by endowing the "material world-soul" with the attributes of an "ideal Divinity," thus giving it an ethical quality. But the Stoic dictum "Live according to nature," which made the cosmic process an ideal for human conduct, did not resolve the ethical issue any more than the doctrines of karma or transmigration.

The philosophers of antiquity occupy the largest part of Huxley's essay, as if to establish the universality and inexorability of the problem. But the account comes to its climax in the modern doctrine of the "ethics of evolution," which might better be called, Huxley suggests, the "evolution of ethics." Unfortunately evolution gives rise to and perpetuates immoral sentiments together with the moral. "Cosmic evolution may teach us how the good and the evil tendencies of man may have come about; but, in itself, it is incompetent to furnish any better reason why what we call good is preferable to what we call evil than we had before." The fallacy in the ethics of evolution is the equation of the "struggle for existence" with the "survival of the fittest," and the assumption that "the fittest" is identical with "the best." But that struggle may favor the worst rather than the best. It is the function of laws and moral precepts to curb the cosmic process, encouraging self-restraint rather than self-assertion, and reminding the individual that he owes to the community, if not existence itself, at least a life better than that of the savage.

> *Social progress means a checking of the cosmic process at every step and the substitution for it of another, which may be called the ethical process; the end of which is not the survival of those who may happen to be the fittest, in respect of the whole of the conditions which obtain, but of those who are ethically the best. . . .*
>
> *Let us understand, once for all, that the ethical progress of society depends, not on imitating the cosmic process, still less in running away from it, but in combating it. It may seem an audacious proposal thus to pit the microcosm against the macrocosm and to set man to subdue nature to his higher ends; but I venture to think that the great intellectual difference between the ancient times with which we have been occupied and our day, lies in the solid foundation we have acquired for the hope that such an enterprise may meet with a certain measure of success. . . .*
>
> *Fragile reed as he may be, man, as Pascal says, is a thinking reed: there lies within him a fund of energy, operating intelligently and so far akin to that which pervades the universe, that it is competent to influence and modify the cosmic process.*

The epigraph introducing "Evolution and Ethics" has the scientist preparing to "cross over" into the enemy camp, that of the moralist. The essay concludes with Huxley, now the scientist-moralist, crossing over into the still more alien camp of the poet – of Tennyson, in his poem "Ulysses," exhorting man "... strong in will / To strive, to seek, to find, and not to yield." Interpolating Tennyson, Huxley reminds us that "we are grown men, and must play the man, cherishing the good that falls in our way, and bearing the evil, in and around us, with stout hearts on diminishing it." The final words of the essay are Tennyson's:

> *It may be that the gulfs will wash us down,*
> *It may be we shall touch the Happy Isles,*
> *... but something ere the end,*
> *Some work of noble note may yet be done.*

This may be too radical a leap for the scientist of our own day – to invoke not only morality but poetry as a corrective to scientism. But he may be reassured by the modest claims made by the poet, and by Huxley himself. If evolution, or any other scientific theory, or nature itself, is not the ultimate arbiter of humanity, not the solution to all of our problems, there may be no single arbiter, no grand theory assuring that morality will triumph. This has not the triumphal appeal of scientism, but it is a salutary, realistic, even scientific appraisal of the human condition.

2014

CHAPTER TWELVE

Einstein:
The Scientist as Pacifist

———————————— ▪ ▮▮▮▮▮ ▪ ————————————

THE CENTENARY OF Albert Einstein's general theory of relativity is an occasion for revisiting that momentous discovery by paying tribute to one of the most famous scientists of modern times. Steven Gimbel has made a welcome contribution to that event with a brief book placing Einstein in his "space and times," as his subtitle has it. "It was relativity," Gimbel declares, "that made Einstein Einstein," giving the scientist the authority (the standing, a jurist might say) to pronounce on public affairs. Sixty years after his death, Einstein still enjoys that authority. An English journal, in a discussion of the war against ISIS, quotes at length (and critically) a 1947 article by Einstein on the Cold War. A *Washington Post* article on the Middle East peace process cites Einstein on the futility of repeated experiments, concluding, "This applies to Gaza."

The biographer of Einstein has to cope with this Einstein – with the posthistory, so to speak, of his hero, who ventured out of his natural terrain and acquired a new persona – as well as the prehistory, the genesis of the ideas that went into the theory that "made Einstein Einstein." The latter is the more challenging because there was little in his background and early years to foresee a theory so novel and abstruse.

Born in 1879 to an assimilated German-Jewish family – the name Albert was a secularized version of Abraham, the grandfather after whom he was named – he was sent to a Catholic school in Munich, where he was the only Jewish child in his class. Bullied by his classmates and harshly treated by the teachers, he hated everything about school and learned, he later insisted, nothing. The high school, the *gymnasium*, was no better. What education he received was from reading on his own and from his uncle, an engineer who introduced him to the mysteries of mathematics. His unruliness and inattentiveness in class and his difficulties with the other students and teachers have given rise to the "myth," as Gimbel puts it, that Einstein was autistic. The myth was not entirely unwarranted. As a child he had "developmental problems" and "issues" with speech, and as a youth he was inept in conversation, socially awkward, inappropriately dressed, and had the affinity for music and visual images rather than language that is characteristic of autism.

After his parents moved first to Milan and then to Pavia, Einstein, at the age of sixteen, left the *gymnasium* in Munich to join them. To continue his studies in German, he applied to the Swiss Federal Institute of Technology in Zurich, but failed the entrance exam; he was admitted the next year upon completing his secondary education at another Swiss school. Neglecting classes, misbehaving, and flouting the social conventions, he barely passed the final exam after four years, scoring next to last. Physics was his favorite and best subject, but, lacking a recommendation from his teachers, he failed to get an assistantship to a physics professor or even a private tutoring job.

The situation became more difficult when his girlfriend, Mileva, a fellow student, got pregnant. She returned to her home in Serbia to give birth to the child, and came back to Zurich leaving the child behind. (This episode was entirely unknown until well after Einstein's death.) In 1901, the offer of a job as a patent clerk in Bern permitted them to marry – an unhappy marriage, as it turned out, although it produced two sons to whom Einstein was devoted. They were eventually divorced, leaving Einstein free to marry (happily, this time) another schoolmate, his cousin Elsa.

In this unlikely atmosphere, Einstein somehow persisted in his study of physics. In a memoir, he explained that his interest in that subject had been inspired by two childhood events. He was four or five when he was shown a compass and realized that the needle always pointed north because it was governed not by any visible or empirical force but by a simple, rational, irrefutable rule. The other epiphany occurred at the age of twelve when he came upon a book on Euclidean geometry, which demonstrated that the intersection of the three altitudes of a triangle in one point, although not on the face of it evident, could be proved without doubt.

"This lucidity and certainty," he recalled, "made an indescribable impression upon me." It was in this spirit, without a professional position or credentials, that he took on the "very revolutionary" project, as he described it, of transforming physics. The theory of relativity in 1905 did just that, overturning the structure of Newtonian physics with a radically new concept of matter and light based purely on reason. Recognition from the scientific community came slower than he would have liked, but it did come, and with it one professorial post after another: in Zurich, Prague, Zurich again, and finally, in 1914, the most prestigious of all, Berlin. It was there, two years later, that he published the general theory of relativity. This is not the place (nor is this reviewer competent) to describe the theory itself, except to commend Steven Gimbel for reconstructing it so lucidly – and in the context of the "space and times" in which Einstein became something more, or other, than the inventor of that theory.

———

It is ironic that Einstein should have returned to Germany at the outset of World War I, remaining there for its duration and beyond. Germany was the country he had denounced as authoritarian and militaristic in his youth, when he publicly tore up his passport and renounced his citizenship. It was the same Einstein who returned, a maverick in science who soon became a maverick in politics. While almost one hundred intellectuals, including some of his colleagues, issued a manifesto supporting the war, Einstein was one of four who signed a counter-manifesto protesting against nationalism and calling for a "universal, world-wide civilization." He also took an active part in an organization promoting a "United States of Europe," which was regarded as sufficiently subversive to be shut down by the government.

Einstein's return to Germany was also the occasion for his asserting himself as a Jew. It was not until then, he later wrote, that "I discovered for the first time that I was a Jew, and I owe this discovery more to Gentiles than Jews." In fact, it came as no discovery; it was just another stage in his recognition of a Jewishness that, in one form or another, had always been with him. Although his family, like so many German Jews, was thoroughly assimilated, his parents were sufficiently respectful of their people and heritage to have a religious relative give the boy lessons about Judaism at home while he was attending a Catholic school. Perhaps as a rebellion against the school, at the age of eight he declared himself an orthodox Jew, committed to observing the Sabbath and the rules of *kashruth*. We are not told if, or how, he managed to keep to that regimen while living in a nonobservant home and going to a Catholic school. In any case, at the *gymnasium* four years later, he deconverted, so to speak. The Euclidean geometry that initiated him into a scientific world governed entirely by reason, reinforced by the reading of popular scientific books, resulted, he later wrote, in a "positively fanatic [orgy of] freethinking," a "suspicion against every kind of authority," and a "skeptical attitude towards the convictions which were alive in any specific social environment."

What he also discovered in Germany was a denigration of Jews, even among scientists and intellectuals, which gave him a heightened appreciation of his Jewishness – not as a religion, to be sure, but as a culture; even, he ventured to say, a nation: "Not until we dare to see ourselves as a nation, not until we respect ourselves, can we gain the respect of others." But it was a special kind of nation he had in mind, defined by morality rather than polity.

> *The bond that has united the Jews for thousands of years and that unites them today is, above all, the democratic ideal of social justice, coupled with the ideal of mutual aid and tolerance among all men. . . . My awareness of the essential nature of Judaism resists the idea of a Jewish state with borders, an army, and a measure of temporal power.*

This was not quite the nationhood most Zionists had in mind. Einstein shared their idea of Palestine as a refuge for persecuted Jews – not, however, as a homeland reserved for them but as a safe area where they could live in peace with their neighbors.

He also valued it as a center of Jewish learning and culture, to exemplify the "intellectual striving" that he saw as the essence of Judaism. It was for this purpose, for the establishment of a Hebrew University, that Einstein exerted all of his efforts. Some of his admirers hoped that he would join the faculty. He never intended to do so, but he did take an active role in fund-raising campaigns. The first of these, a much-publicized trip in 1921 with Chaim Weizmann, the head of the World Zionist Organization, brought him to New York, where he discovered what, for him, was a new breed of Jews, Eastern European immigrants: "These men and women still retain a healthy national feeling; it has not yet been destroyed by the process of atomization and dispersion. I found these people extraordinarily ready for self-sacrifice and practically creative."

A visit to Palestine two years later introduced him to two other varieties of Jews: the "incredibly lively people" of Tel Aviv, who had created out of nothing "a modern Hebrew city with busy economic and intellectual life," and, in painful contrast, the people in Jerusalem praying at the Western Wall, "dull-minded tribal companions ... men with a past but without a future." In this context, "tribal" sounds pejorative, but it is entirely favorable applied to the settlers as a whole: "I greatly liked my tribal companions in Palestine, as farmers, as workers, and as citizens." The land was not very fertile and would not accommodate very many Jews, but colonization would succeed in making the country a "moral center."

———

While Einstein's reputation was being acclaimed abroad (and rewarded with generous lecture fees), life in Germany was becoming more disagreeable, the antisemitism more overt. His work was denounced, even by some of his colleagues, as "Jewish science." In 1931 he began to spend winter semesters at the California Institute of Technology. He was there, in January 1933, when Hitler took power, and he never returned to Germany. For Einstein, as for so many German Jews, the United States became a place of refuge. He was especially pleased to receive an offer to join the newly founded Institute for Advanced Study in Princeton, which was devoted entirely to theoretical science. It was there, as a resident scholar and American citizen, that he spent the rest of his life.

But it was not a tranquil life, for once again Einstein found himself at odds with his colleagues at home and with associates abroad. While he was developing a unified field theory that would advance upon the general theory, quantum mechanics was taking physics in a new direction. So, too, his relation to the Zionist movement became problematic with the emergence of Revisionist Zionism, which sought just that statehood he had forsworn and which was prepared to use military force to achieve it. The new Zionism violated not only Einstein's sense of a proper, peaceful Zionism but also his vision of a proper, peaceful world order. Earlier, in response to the threat of the First World War, he had declared himself a pacifist. Now, Zionism and pacifism were at a crossroads, and his Zionism lost on two counts – because it was nationalistic as well as militaristic. Yet his esteem among Zionists was such that at the death of President Weizmann in 1952, Prime Minister David Ben-Gurion offered the presidency of Israel to Einstein, in spite of their differences. Einstein graciously thanked him and firmly declined.

Pacifism created problems for Einstein with his fellow scientists as well. Worried at the prospect of atomic weapons wielded by Nazis, he wrote and cosigned a letter to President Roosevelt in 1939 urging America to take the initiative in nuclear research. But he did not seek to be involved in what became the Manhattan Project, and was not invited to do so, largely because of his political views – his pacifism, primarily, but also his advocacy of socialism as against the "anarchy" and immorality of capitalism. (He was high on J. Edgar Hoover's subversive list for both reasons.) He supported World War II as "morally justified" against Nazi aggression, but he also vigorously supported the cause of conscientious objectors. And he opposed the Cold War with the Soviet Union as a war for nuclear supremacy that might well end with the "annihilation of all life on earth." (He later regretted writing that letter to Roosevelt.)

Einstein was not an innocent preaching the virtues of pacifism. On at least one occasion he expressed qualms about it. Gimbel mentions Freud, in passing, as having a novel "picture of the human mind," and as one of those Einstein proposed for a larger role in the Hebrew University. (They were both members of the university's first board of governors.) More notable is a public exchange of letters between them in 1932. A private note accompanying Einstein's letter suggests that he had read Freud's *Civilization and Its Discontents*, published two years earlier, which elaborated upon the "death instinct" that played so large a part in the human psyche.

It was this theory that prompted Einstein's query: "Is there any way of delivering mankind from the menace of war?" As one "immune from nationalist bias," he told Freud, his own answer was simple: the establishment of "a legislative and judicial body to settle every conflict arising between nations." This was no mean goal, for it would require the unconditional surrender by every nation of its liberty – "its sovereignty, that is to say." This raised other questions. Why was it that men succumbed with "such wild enthusiasm" to wars that could cost them their lives? Could it be that there was, in man, "a lust for hatred and destruction" that would induce that ultimate sacrifice? Finally, there was the practical question: "Is it possible to control man's mental evolution so as to make him proof against the psychosis of hate and destructiveness?" He was speaking, he hastened to add, not only of the "so-called uncultured masses" but of the "so-called intelligentsia" as well, who were just as apt to yield to that "collective psychosis."

Freud's response was hardly reassuring. Reminding Einstein of his own recent work on that subject, he regretfully concluded that "there is no likelihood of suppressing humanity's aggressive tendencies." Any attempt to replace brute force by the ideal of right was doomed to fail because "right is founded on brute force and even today needs violence to maintain it." There was another question that intrigued him and, he hoped, would not shock Einstein: "Why do we, you and I and many others, protest so vehemently against war, instead of just accepting it as another of life's odious importunities?" Freud's own answer might have surprised, even shocked, Einstein:

> *With pacifists like us, it is not merely an intellectual and affective repulsion, but a constitutional intolerance, an idiosyncrasy in its most drastic form. And it would seem that the aesthetic ignominies of warfare play almost as large a part in this repugnance as war's atrocities.*

Pacifism as an "idiosyncrasy," an "intellectual" and "aesthetic" repulsion against the "ignominies" of war – this was not Einstein's pacifism, and certainly not a pacifism that might appeal to the "intelligentsia," let alone the "uncultured masses."

Freud concluded by apologizing to Einstein for a letter that would surely disappoint him. Einstein, in turn, thanked Freud for a "truly classic . . . altogether magnificent" letter, and for his courage in pursuing the truth and professing his convictions. That response was dated December 3, 1932. By the time the correspondence was published the following year, Hitler was in power and Einstein was in exile. Two thousand copies of *Warum Krieg?* (*Why War?*) were published in German and another two thousand in English. Einstein may have been disappointed but not deterred. Pacifism continued to be one of his major public causes.

———◆———

Einstein had come a long way from the physicist to the social activist. It is as if, displaced by quantum mechanics from the center of physics, he found a new calling in politics. But perhaps not entirely a new calling, for he was now seeking a rationality in society akin to the reason he had so passionately sought in physics. A famous quotation from Einstein is his response to a rabbi who asked him whether he believed in God: "I believe in Spinoza's God who reveals himself in the harmony of all Being, not in a God who concerns himself with the fate and actions of man." The rabbi was pleased to think of this as "a scientific formula for monotheism." Another reading would see it as an invitation to Einstein to fill the vacuum by doing what Spinoza's God wisely refrained from doing: bringing harmony to mankind and rationalizing a vexingly irrational world.

To a critic today, some of Einstein's views, on war and peace, capitalism and socialism, Judaism and Zionism, may appear as almost a parody of the right-minded (which is to say, left-thinking) progressive of his time. Steven Gimbel is relatively benign about this Einstein, the public intellectual, out of respect for the scientist who "made Einstein Einstein." But the social effects of the spirit that animated him – his passion for a rationalism that is productive in science but all too often counterproductive in society – are perhaps not so benign.

2015

CHAPTER THIRTEEN

Trilling: The Moral Imagination, Properly Understood

WHEN LIONEL TRILLING died in 1975, he was not only the most eminent literary critic in America, but also, some would argue, the most eminent intellectual figure. Three years before his death, he received the first of the Thomas Jefferson Awards, the highest honor the federal government confers for "distinguished intellectual achievement in the humanities." Today, his name is unknown even to graduate students of English literature. More disquieting, the mode of thought that was uniquely his is not so much in disfavor as simply ignored – not even a matter of contention.

Trilling, who was so sensitive a recorder of the culture, may have anticipated this turn in his own reputation as well as the culture. His Jefferson Lecture, "Mind in the Modern World," was exhortatory rather than celebratory, cautioning about tendencies in the culture apparent to him although not yet to many others, which had the effect of diminishing the force and legitimacy of mind. He did not use the words "postmodernism" or "deconstruction" – they were not in common usage then – but that was what he had in mind when he deplored the increasingly esoteric and dehumanizing, as he thought it, nature of the humanistic disciplines.

That disrespect for mind he saw epitomized in the aggressive relativism that ridiculed the very idea of "objectivity," and with it, Trilling insisted, the idea of reality itself. Today, Trilling's defense of objectivity, as an idea and an ideal, has a prophetic ring, an appeal to redemption, so to speak. "In the face of the certainty that the effort of objectivity will fall short of what it aims at," he told his audience, "those who undertake to make the effort do so out of something like a sense of intellectual honor and out of the faith that in the practical life, which includes the moral life, some good must follow from even the relative success of the endeavor."

"The practical life, which includes the moral life" – and the intellectual and aesthetic life as well. In an age that is as skeptical about morality as it is about objectivity, Trilling's insistent sense of morality – "moral realism," he called it – can well be derided as Victorian. Indeed, it was from one of the most notable Victorians that he imbibed that sense. An intellectual biography of Matthew Arnold was his first work, and the spirit of Arnold, "literature as a criticism of life," hovers over all of his work, extending far beyond the Victorians and engaging the most disparate writers and thinkers: George Orwell and Isaac Babel, Mark Twain and T. S. Eliot, Wordsworth and Hemingway, Jane Austen and Rudyard Kipling, Henry James and James Joyce, Sigmund Freud and E. M. Forster.

In a series of lectures published as *Sincerity and Authenticity*, he went further still. Philosophers ancient and modern – Plato and Aristotle, Rousseau and Hegel, Nietzsche and Sartre – mingled with poets, novelists, writers and thinkers of every genre, and even the occasional historical figure. The juxtaposition of characters and ideas is exhilarating and sometimes startling. A discussion of Rousseau's idea of sincerity, for example, prompts the thought: "Oratory and the novel: which is to say, Robespierre and Jane Austen" – an odd coupling, Trilling observes: "This, I fancy, is the first time the two personages have ever been brought together in a single sentence, separated from each other by nothing more than the conjunction that links them." But they are not, he insists, "factitiously conjoined. They are consanguineous, each is in lineal descent from Rousseau, cousins-german through their commitment to the 'honest soul' and its appropriate sincerity." The ideas of sincerity and authenticity are also "conjoined" as moral concepts, each with its distinctive lineage, authenticity suggesting "a more strenuous moral experience than sincerity does, a more exigent conception of the self and of what being true to it consists in, a wider reference to the universe and man's place in it, and a less acceptant and genial view of the social circumstances of life."

It was Edmund Burke who introduced the term "moral imagination" into political discourse. But it was Trilling (who read Burke although perhaps not closely enough to have picked up on that phrase) who popularized it and made it the heart of his literary and social criticism. Trilling is sometimes criticized for being unduly subtle, complicated, oblique. But that is because those are the characteristics of the moral imagination "properly understood" (as Tocqueville would have said). Trilling is also sometimes criticized for being conservative, in spite of his often quoted statement that today "there are no conservative or reactionary ideas in general circulation." That statement was made in 1950, in the preface to *The Liberal Imagination*, and was followed by the comment (rarely quoted) that there were, nevertheless, conservative "impulses," which were "certainly very strong, perhaps even stronger than most of us know." Moreover, the book itself was a critique of the "liberal imagination," which did not appreciate the complexity of moral life and therefore of social and political life. More than half a century later, Trilling's moral imagination stands as a corrective to the "terrible simplifiers" who have ideologized our culture as well as our polity.

2009

Of This Time, Of That Place

CHAPTER FOURTEEN

American Democracy
and Its European Critics

━━━━━■IIIII■━━━━━

W HEN DICKENS visited America in 1842, he heard an American refer to England as "that unnat'ral old parent." Today it is more often the Englishman who is heard to complain of America as an unnatural offspring. Filial relations are difficult in any case, but the cultural hostility that seems at present to exist between America and England (between America and all Europe, in fact) is such as to require special explanation.

In the mid-nineteenth century, with the memory of the revolutionary struggle still fresh, recriminations and counter-recriminations between the old country and the new played a large part in international discourse. Exulting in its democratic institutions and pioneer vigor, America taunted the old monarchies of Europe for their decadent aristocracies and effete cultures. Europe, in return, was contemptuous of the primitiveness and crudity of the erstwhile colony.

For every American who thought the Declaration of Independence was a new dispensation in the history of Western civilization, there were several Europeans who echoed Sydney

Smith's famous derisive inquiry: "Who reads an American book?" A Frenchman writing of America in the 1850s was congratulated for his resourcefulness when he announced a chapter on the *beaux arts* in America and followed it with a blank leaf. Matthew Arnold's attitude to American statesmen was typical of European opinion: Lincoln – shrewd, sagacious, humorous, honest, courageous – all the qualities deserving of the most sincere esteem and praise, but he had not, Arnold regretted, "distinction." Washington, who admittedly had distinction, Arnold persisted in regarding as an Englishman who accidentally happened to reside in America. "America is not interesting," Arnold decided, and Europe concurred.

To make matters worse, this lowliness of the American culture and character was taken as a measure of the ignobility of American politics. That democracy was an "aristocracy of blackguards" was a sentiment variously attributed to Talleyrand and Byron, and mouthed by generations of Europeans. Macaulay was not the first to warn that liberty and civilization would be destroyed in the chaos of American democracy: "Either the poor would plunder the rich and civilization would perish, or order and prosperity would be saved by a strong military government and liberty would perish." Tocqueville's memorable work, *Democracy in America*, gave currency to the expression "the tyranny of the majority," and not until the appearance of Lord Bryce's *American Commonwealth*, exactly half a century later, did anyone seriously challenge the justice or the relevance of the *bon mot*. It was Matthew Arnold who declared, "States are saved by their righteous remnant," and thereby pronounced sentence of death on America, for in America, most Europeans were assured, there was no saving remnant, no enlightened minority, only an ignorant and omnipotent majority.

But these, American patriots consoled themselves, were the

views of Europe's benighted conservatives and Whigs. The harassed and oppressed radicals in Europe, they were confident, would approve of America's glorious experiment in democracy. Dickens, for example, who in England seemed to be playing the part of an American, a breaker of ancestral images, was expected to lend his prestige to the American cause. Dickens himself eagerly looked forward to his visit to America in 1842. He was prepared to believe that all Americans were free men and that freedom was a precious thing. Yet, while in England he had been amused by the vulgarities of the lower classes, he found that in America he was repelled by the spitting, tobacco-chewing boors who did not know the proper use of the pocket handkerchief or the rules governing the dining table. He was distressed that American tradesmen sometimes neglected to remove their hats in the presence of their betters, that the White House was periodically desecrated by the hordes of people who were indiscriminately shown through it, that the barrister's wig and gown had been discarded, and that all social barriers were let down until the very word "gentleman" no longer existed. Although his plebeian soul waxed indignant at the thought of slavery and he resolved not to accept tributes from the South, he was so taken with Southern gentility that he found himself attending public dinners there. It was, in the end, not slavery so much as spitting that offended him. "I tremble for a radical coming here," Dickens later remarked, fearing that unless he was a staunch radical indeed he would "return home a Tory."

Dickens was the first of a long procession of visitors whose radicalism seemed to desert them upon disembarking on America's shores. English reformers who spent their lives trying to abolish the degrading institution of the debtor's prison, who were full of compassion for the starved wrecks of human beings inhabiting the London slums, and who despised the gross inequities of English society that made of one class the lackey of another, came to America and promptly fell to criticizing the American masses for their materialism, their wealth, and their love of comforts. "It would be well," Dickens wrote, "for the American people as a whole, if they loved the Real less and the Ideal somewhat more." Yet it is interesting to notice that the burden of Dickens's lectures and conversations revolved about the gross reality of the American copyright laws, which permitted the circulation of pirated editions of his work and so deprived him of his royalties.

Given to their own peculiar variety of idealism, Americans, in turn, were offended by the exhibition of a writer – and a prosperous one at that – laboring so tiresomely the issue of money. However, they soon forgave him the cruel portrait of America in *Martin Chuzzlewit* and welcomed him enthusiastically on his second tour of America twenty-five years later. A net profit of over $100,000 on that occasion may have helped reconcile Dickens to America and determined him to have a postscript added to all future editions of *Martin Chuzzlewit* and *American Notes* testifying to "the changes in the graces and amenities of life" in America.

Tobacco-chewing has given way in our time to gum-chewing, and spitting is disappearing, while handkerchiefs have made their appearance and other minor improvements have been effected in American manners. On the other hand, the giant Coca-Cola dispenser is as conspicuous an eyesore as was the cuspidor; and the question "Who reads an American book?" has been replaced by "Who sees an American movie?" – with an answer even more disturbing to the European of taste and culture. Once it was only visitors to America who were affronted by the visible evidence of the American common man. Today, with American culture becoming a universal phenomenon, all of Europe's self-designated guardians of civilization profess anxiety and dismay.

When a Tory clergyman or schoolmaster addresses the editor of *The Times* to denounce America because of its insidious corruption of the English language, or when a French Catholic conservative, in *Le Figaro*, anathematizes America for the heresy of confounding human progress with material progress, no one need be surprised. It is the privilege of the conservative to be wary of cultural and social innovations. But when these voices are joined by those of professed radicals writing in the *New Statesman and Nation* and *Les Temps Modernes*, the American has reason to be annoyed. He is reminded of Dickens, who was full of love for the common people until he came to meet them as rulers in their native habitat.

Like Dickens, most European radical intellectuals have not had much opportunity to appreciate how common the common man can be if he is given his head. The fact is that their own countries are democracies only on the surface. In France and England democracy came as an afterthought, as a political veneer covering the social and cultural accretions of many generations of aristocracy.

In England particularly, where socialists pride themselves on their "advanced" institutions, most of the symbols of class distinction persist: ways of speech recalling the playing fields of Eton or the streets of the East End of London, the worker's cap and the gentleman's hat, the peculiar manners and morals associated with each social class. The House of Lords may be divested of political power, the aristocracy weaned away from the luxurious habits of a more affluent age, and ancient estates converted into national museums for the edification and satisfaction of the lower classes. But culturally, England remains as it always was – Disraeli's "two nations." (A good case can be made for the existence of three: when the middle class finally learned to say "port" instead of "port wine," the aristocracy promptly shifted from "port" to "port wine.") Professor D. W. Brogan observed that while in America all the resources of snob-appeal advertising have perpetually to be engaged in the creation and repair of the social fences, in England the social fences are wild hedges that grow even when left alone. And among the most important social fences that are native to England, but not to America, are the cultural barriers separating the social classes.

The English radical intellectual, himself generally a product of one of the respectable "public" schools, is effectively confined within those cultural barriers. He is a firm believer in the right of the people to determine public legislation, control industry, and administer the state in their own interests. But he is also firmly convinced that the popular press is despicable and that in matters of culture there must be no pampering of the common, vulgar mind. When it comes to books, the cinema, radio, and television, he insists upon giving the people what is good for them rather than what they may happen to want. And he knows what is good. When it was the fashion to do so, he denounced the classical, aristocratic, High Church traditions of English society; but he is still, as the saying goes, living off the capital of an earlier age. Nothing pleases a Labour MP more than to expose the faulty Latin of the honorable gentleman on the opposite bench. And no feature of the *New Statesman and Nation* is more scintillating than the "weekend competitions" in which good radicals vie with each other in producing mock-heroic verse in iambic pentameter or elegies in the Greek manner.

———

America, so wealthy in other respects, has no cultural or social capital to fall back on. It must create resources as it goes along, and the resulting improvisation is often painfully obvious. There has been no leisure class to build up a fund of classical learning, graceful living, pleasant manners, and high thoughts. Its culture has had to be hastily assembled from the only natural resources available to it – from the democratic, egalitarian, commercial spirit. "High culture" in America does exist and is probably the equal of the upper-class Englishman's culture, but it is not a significant social fact. It exists in the interstices of society; it is the idiosyncrasy of an individual rather than the accepted feature of a class. The only culture of any significance in America is "popular culture," which is all too fittingly named. The book of the month, the movie of the week, and the current issue of *Life* magazine are the cultural staples of all Americans. They are as much a part of the typical American's equipment (and "typical" is a more meaningful concept in this country than elsewhere) as the current slang expression, popular song, or fashion craze.

The European intellectual, radical or otherwise, has little sympathy or patience with this popular culture, particularly when it threatens to invade his own domain. The radical, however, has the obligation of accounting for it in such a way, preferably, as not to reflect upon the virtues of democracy, to which he is politically committed. He then has two possible lines of argument open to him. He can argue, in the fashion of the eighteenth-century radical, that there is an integral relationship between democracy on the one hand and science, intelligence, and public enlightenment on the other. The democracy par excellence in this view is the Republic of Letters, the rationally organized and rational-thinking society that would inevitably arise once the oppressive institutions of authoritarian church and despotic state were abolished. If America can hardly aspire to the title of a Republic of Letters, it is only because its democracy is faulty. And since it is patently neither a monarchy nor a theocracy – the latter having been effectively disposed of and the remaining influential priests being occupied in preaching the unecclesiastical gospel of happiness – it can only be an oligarchy.

Another possible line of argument ends at the same point, although it starts a century later with the Marxist doctrine. To the Marxist, democracy is not a respectable analytic concept. The fact that a country is or is not democratic cannot be taken as an adequate explanation of any social or cultural situation. The explanation must be in terms of the economic structure of society. The nature of American culture, then, can be accounted for only by the nature of American capitalism. Whether the European radical derives from the tradition of the Enlightenment or from the tradition of Marxism, his conclusion is the same: American popular culture is the product of American capitalism.

To accept the image of America as reflected in the pages of the *New Statesman* and *Les Temps Modernes* is to believe not only that American culture is depraved and vicious but that it is part of a conspiracy deliberately to degrade the American people. Hollywood is not merely dedicated to the ignoble purpose of making a lot of money quickly. It is dedicated to the still more unworthy object of propping up the sinking foundations of capitalism. It has been given the job, by the agents of Big Business, of manufacturing soporifics designed to dull the minds of the dissatisfied masses, and stimulants to brutalize them so as to direct their aggressions against each other instead of against their overlords. United in conspiracy with Hollywood are the other instruments of popular culture: the sensation-seeking press, the bare-bosomed heroines and gun-toting heroes of fiction, the women's magazines with their multicolored pictures of domestic felicity in the form of shiny kitchen sinks, the radio soap operas able to induce catharsis on a mass scale and at small cost.

This conception of America is developed at great length in the writings of Harold Laski, and especially in *The American Democracy* (1948). Laski posed the question all Europeans ask: Why is there in America such a depressing uniformity of values, a single species of Babbittry that defies geographical and historical variations, and that makes of Robert Lynd's Middletown a portrait in miniature of any American metropolis? His answer is typical of European radicals: the incubus of Big Business lies heavily upon the whole country, stifling individual expression and corrupting individual tastes. Why do the three great media of public communications – the press, the cinema, and the radio – frequently distort the truth and almost always refrain from telling the whole truth? Because they are interested not in the truth but in profits, and they will say only what it is profitable to say. And, since profits in the long run depend upon the continuation of the profit system, it is the virtues of the system that must be sold as well as the virtues of the actual commodities advertised.

Europeans have not always answered the question thus. Tocqueville, whose great work *Democracy in America* appeared more than a century before Laski's effort, is still a more reliable guide to America than his successor. If American society is standardized, he reasoned, it is not because society is dominated by the entrepreneur scheming to direct all of society for his ulterior ends, but because it is dominated by the common man, to whom the values of Babbittry are naturally congenial. It is precisely because the dispensers of popular culture are interested only in making profits that they give the public what it wants. American mass society is the product of American democracy. The only significant tyranny in America is the tyranny of the majority.

To anyone familiar with American life, or even to anyone with a genuine respect for the facts of history and the logic of the argument, Tocqueville's thesis is more persuasive then Laski's. It has been said of Tocqueville, with some justice, that he tended to attribute to democracy the consequences of industrial civilization. So it may be said of Laski, with more justice, that he tended to attribute to capitalism the consequences of democracy. When Coca-Cola, comic books, and Raymond Chandler murder mysteries invaded Europe, penetrating even into the British stronghold, radicals set up a great cry against American capitalism. What they chose not to see is that the real offender is not capitalism so much as the European masses, who have given an enthusiastic reception to these supposedly degenerate products of capitalist America. Europe's real complaint against America is not that America is exporting capitalist culture, but that it is exporting popular culture. This the European radical cannot bring himself to admit. He is so painfully aware that popular culture is not what he was educated to regard as culture that he would like to forget how genuinely popular it is. Even the materialism that Laski cites as proof of the oligarchic character of American society may be taken as evidence of its essentially democratic nature.

Henry James, the prototype of the expatriate, listed those items of "high civilization" that America lacked: state, sovereign, church, clergy, army, diplomatic service, country gentlemen, palaces, manors, parsonages, thatched cottages, ivied ruins, cathedrals, little Norman churches, and great universities. The European, he continued, believes that if these things are left out, everything is left out. But the American knows that a good deal remains. "What it is that remains – that is his secret, his joke, as one might say."

The joke, or "joker," in America is democracy. For good or ill, democracy has fashioned the American culture. Lord Bryce once explained why American democracy is not better than it is: because it is so good. One might say the same of the American culture. If there were not a sense of equality, there might be an aristocracy of the intellect. If there were not a sense of material expansiveness, there might be a keener sense of spirituality. If popular culture were not so accessible to all men, perhaps high culture would be more accessible to the few. If Americans did not excel in quantity, they might be more proficient in quality. To a British visitor in America, Oliver Wendell Holmes remarked: "We should find it very hard to match five thousand American gentlemen with five thousand English; but we could match five million ordinary Americans against the same number of your countrymen without fear of the result."

This is the "joker" in America. Democracy, it turns out, while not conducive to the noble virtues of art, mind, and manner – perhaps *because* it is not conducive to these virtues – has its own virtues of tolerance, sympathy, and well-being. If it cannot boast the civilization or sensibility of the great aristocratic ages of the past, it can boast a civilization and sensibility of its own, in which things of the heart take precedence over things of the mind, kindness is more prominent than heroism, and goodwill more conspicuous than good manners. American democracy may not lay claim to the virtues of European culture, but neither need it confess to the vices of poverty and servility which still plague much of European society. And as Europe becomes Americanized, perhaps America will find itself assuming some of the cultural qualities of Europe. In a new world becoming old, democracy and culture may yet find a new level, a happier balance.

1952

CHAPTER FIFTEEN

Democratic Remedies
for Democratic Disorders

———————■ ❚❚❚❚ ■———————

A FAMOUS PASSAGE in *The Federalist Papers* calls for "a republican remedy for the diseases most incident to republican government." The diseases the Founding Fathers had in mind were those associated with factions: the pursuit of special interests to the detriment of the general interest. And the main remedy they proposed was federalism: the general interest to be represented in the national legislature, local and particular interests in the state legislatures.

Today, it is our democratic society, rather than our republican government, that is problematic. And the diseases incident to that society are moral and cultural rather than political: the collapse of ethical principles and habits, the loss of respect for authorities and institutions, the breakdown of the family, the decline of civility, the vulgarization of high culture, and the degradation of popular culture. Three-quarters of the people in a recent poll said that the main cause of America's problems is "moral decay."

In their most virulent form these diseases manifest themselves in illegitimacy, crime, violence, drug addiction, illiteracy,

pornography, and welfare dependency. Some of these conditions have improved in recent years, but there is little cause for
complacency. If the number of births to teenagers has decreased,
the proportion of out-of-wedlock births, to adults as well as
teenagers, continues to increase – and this country still has the
dubious distinction of having the highest rate of teenage preg-
nancy in the industrialized world. If divorce is tapering off, it is
because cohabitation is becoming so common; people living
together without benefit of marriage can separate without benefit of divorce, and do so with greater facility and frequency. If
there are fewer abortions, it is in part because illegitimacy has
become more respectable. Indeed, the term "illegitimacy" is
taboo; the preferred terms in official circles are "nonmarital
childbearing" or "alternative mode of parenting." If one drug
falls out of favor, another takes its place, and the decline in drug
use among adults is more than offset by an increase among
progressively younger people. And in spite of the recent decrease
of crime (which, penologists warn us, may be reversed when
today's baby boomers become tomorrow's delinquents), teenage boys, regardless of race, are still more likely to die from gun-
shot wounds than from all natural causes combined, and
homicide is the second leading cause of death for all young
people and the leading cause for young blacks.

From a longer perspective, even the good news may give us
pause. The decline or stabilization of some of the indices of
social disarray does not begin to bring us back to the status
quo ante – that now-maligned period of the 1950s before the
precipitous rise of those indices. With a divorce rate more than
twice that of the 1950s, half of the marriages today, and well
over half of the remarriages, are expected to end in divorce.
Illegitimacy has increased sixfold, and the number of children
living with one parent has risen from less than one-tenth to

more than one-quarter. The rate of violent crime, although considerably lower than it was only a few years ago, is still almost four times that of the 1950s. And the much-heralded reduction of the percentage of families on AFDC has brought us down from five times that of the 1950s to three and one-half times.

If some of the good news is only equivocally good, some of the bad news is unequivocally bad. The escalating violence on TV, the ready accessibility of pornography and sexual perversions on the Internet, the "dumbing down" of education at all levels, and the "defining down" of deviancy of every kind – these too are part of the social pathology of our time. And this pathology, which affects not only the "underclass" but the entire population, shows no signs of abating; on the contrary, the diseases are becoming more acute and more pervasive. Affluence and education, we have discovered, provide no immunity from moral and cultural disorders.

This situation is all the more distressing because it violates two of our most cherished assumptions: that moral progress is a necessary byproduct of material progress, and that enlightened legislation will solve our social ills. The 1960s witnessed both an expanding economy and a heightened social consciousness. Yet it was precisely then (for reasons abundantly analyzed elsewhere) that the "moral statistics," as the Victorians called them, took a turn for the worse. And not only in this country but in most Western countries, which is why the Vietnam War is not the crucial factor it has sometimes been made out to be. If single parenthood or welfare dependency do not preoccupy most Europeans (with the notable exception of the English), this is more a reflection of the permissive ethos in their countries than of the objective conditions. And if Americans are more acutely aware of these conditions, if we perceive them as serious social problems, it is because we pride ourselves on being not only the most democratic nation but also the most moral one. ("Moralistic," our denigrators would say.) Thus we are preternaturally alert to the moral diseases incident to democratic society and anxious to find democratic remedies for those diseases.

One remedy looks to the most democratic branch of the government, the legislature, to pass laws designed to promote the moral well-being of the country (income-tax measures favoring married couples) or to nullify those laws that have contributed to our ill-being ("no-fault" divorce laws that facilitate and may encourage divorce). Another remedy is the devolution of power from the federal government to state and local governments, on the theory that the latter reflect the moral temper of the people more faithfully than the remote Washington bureaucracy; this is the rationale behind the 1996 welfare-reform bill making the states responsible for relief. A more radical remedy looks to the Constitution for redress – an amendment, for example, to forbid or limit abortion.

These are all efforts to find political remedies for our social and moral disorders, A nonpolitical remedy has also been proposed, to near-universal acclaim. This is the restoration and revitalization of civil society: families, communities, churches, civic and cultural organizations. It is an attractive idea because it calls upon nothing more than such natural, familiar, universal institutions as families and communities. Moreover, it is preeminently a democratic idea. It is democracy on the smallest scale – the "little platoon" that Burke described as "the first principle (the germ as it were) of public affections." It is also an attribute of democracy on the largest scale – Tocqueville's "voluntary associations," which have the crucial task of mediating between the individual and the state. In addition, it serves as a corrective to that other democratic flaw identified by Tocqueville: "the tyranny of the majority," the power of the collective mass of the people which may be inimical to the liberty of individuals and minorities.

Today, civil society is asked to assume yet another task: that of repairing the moral fabric of democratic society. The institutions of civil society, we are told, are the "seedbeds of virtue." It is here, in families and communities, that individual character takes shape, that children become civilized and socialized, that people acquire a sense of social as well as individual responsibility, that self-interest is reconciled with the general interest, and that civility mutes the discord of opposing wills. And all of this is achieved naturally, organically, without the artificial contrivances of government, without the passage of laws or the intrusion of bureaucracies, without recourse to the coercive, punitive power of the state.

It sounds too good to be true. And it is too good to be true. The intentions of the proponents of civil society are admirable, and today more than ever the idea of a mediating structure between an unrestrained individualism and an overweening state is commendable. The difficulty is that civil society – not as it once was, as Burke or Tocqueville or even our parents (or ourselves, of a certain age) knew it, but as it now is – cannot bear the burden of the charge placed upon it. Civil society has been described as an "immune system against cultural disease." But the fact is that much of civil society has been infected by the same virus that produced that disease: the ethical and cultural relativism that reduces all values, all standards, and all authority to expressions of personal will and inclination. Even the family, the traditional bedrock of civil society, has not been spared. Civil society, then, is a necessary but not a sufficient remedy for the diseases incident to democratic society.

———

When the Founding Fathers devised a "new science of politics" based upon the principle of divided powers and interests, they understood that this "science" alone was insufficient to sustain a proper republican government, that the best political arrangements were of no avail in the absence of "virtue and wisdom." Madison wrote, "I go on this great republican principle, that the people will have virtue and intelligence to select men of virtue and wisdom.... To suppose that any form of government will secure liberty or happiness without any virtue in the people, is a chimerical idea."

Tocqueville, visiting America half a century later, found that a democracy, even more than a republic, is threatened by an egalitarianism that undermines liberty and an individualism that saps "the spring of public virtues." America's saving grace was the proliferation of the "voluntary associations" that mitigate the worst effects of democracy and maintain a sense of public virtue. Among the most important of these associations were the churches. When he first came to the United States, he had been struck by the "religious atmosphere of the country," where religion and freedom coexisted in great harmony – so different from the situation in France, where they seemed to be "almost always marching in opposite directions." It was religion in the service of virtue that made freedom possible. And American religion was uniquely able to do this because it was not an established religion. Americans cherished the idea of religious freedom, the separation of church and state, as much as they cherished their particular church or sect. Religion was "the first of their political institutions" precisely because it was not, strictly speaking, a political institution at all.

Again and again, Tocqueville reflected upon the relationship of religion to morality and of both to freedom:

> *While the law allows the American people to do everything, there are things which religion prevents them from imagining and forbids them to dare.*
>
> *Freedom sees religion as the companion of its struggles and triumphs, the cradle of its infancy, and the divine source of its rights. Religion is considered as the guardian of mores, and mores are regarded as the guarantee of the laws and pledge for the maintenance of freedom itself.*
>
> *Despotism may be able to do without faith, but freedom cannot. Religion is much more needed in ... [a] republic ... than in ... [a] monarchy ... and in democratic republics most of all. How could society escape destruction if, when political ties are relaxed, moral ties are not tightened? And what can be done with a people master of itself if it is not subject to God?*

Tocqueville anticipated the objection commonly heard today that this view of religion is demeaning, even irreligious, because it is concerned more with the utility of religion than with its spirituality. "I do not know," he admitted, "if all Americans have faith in their religion – for who can read the secrets of the heart? – but I am sure that they think it necessary for the maintenance of republican institutions." Every religion, he noted, has two dimensions: one that elevates the soul above the material and sensory world, and another that imposes upon each man an obligation to mankind. These are complementary functions, and both are essential for the self-government that is at the heart of democracy.

———

Like Tocqueville, a visitor to the United States today may well be struck by the "religious atmosphere of the country." He will also be struck (again, like Tocqueville) by the conspicuous contrast between the United States and Europe. In most European countries, there is an inverse relation between religious commitment and education; the least educated tend to be the most religious. In the United States, there is a high level of both education and religion. In the United States, 43 percent attend church at least weekly; in Britain, 14 percent; in France, 12 percent; in Sweden, 4 percent. In the United States, 49 percent say that religion is very important in their lives; in Britain, 17 percent; in France, 10 percent; in Sweden, 0 percent. The French press was startled by the million or so young people who flooded Paris in August 1997 to hear Pope John Paul II celebrate Mass on World Youth Day. But only half of French youth even call themselves Catholic (compared with almost 90 percent who did so three decades ago), and fewer than half of these practice their faith. At a conference in Prague about the same time, the president of the Czech Republic, Václav Havel, defined the central problem of our time as "global atheism" and called for a revival of those values and principles that all religions hold in common.

America is notably exempt from that "global atheism." "The churching of America," as sociologists call it, is reflected in a variety of statistics, some almost incredible. A staggering 96 percent of Americans profess to believe in God or a "universal spirit" and 90 percent in heaven. (In good American fashion, only 65 percent believe in the devil and 73 percent in hell.) Sixty-seven percent identify themselves as members of a church; 60 percent say they attend church at least once a month, and 43 percent that they had attended in the previous week; 90 percent say that they pray at least once a week and 75 percent daily. With only small variations, these statistics hold for the better-educated and the less-educated, for the rich and the poor. Indeed, those earning more than $75,000 a year are more likely to have attended religious services in the previous week than those earning less than $15,000. It may well be that people are reporting what they think they ought to be doing rather than what they actually do. But this too is significant, reflecting values that are believed in even though they may not be observed in practice.

Other statistics demonstrate the social effects of religious affiliation and observance. The practice of religion has a high correlation with family stability, communal activity, and charitable contributions; and a low correlation with suicide, depression, drug addiction, alcoholism, and crime. Black Protestants and white Catholics, with similarly high church attendance, have similarly low divorce rates. Those who seldom or never attend church have seven times the cohabitation rate of those who do. (This spills over into the following generation; children whose mothers frequently attend services are half as likely to cohabit in adulthood as those whose mothers are not church-goers.) Not "safe sex" but the regular practice of religion is one of the most important factors in preventing out-of-wedlock births. Religion has even been shown to be conducive to physical well-being. Regular church attendance is correlated with lower mortality rates from heart, liver, and lung diseases. Older adults who attend church regularly are twice as likely to have strong immune systems as those who do not.

These comforting statistics about religion would seem to be at odds with the discomforting ones about our social and moral condition. If religion is so important in America, and if it seems to have such positive effects, why is the country in the state of moral decay reported by so many people? The anomaly may be accounted for, in large part, by the changing character of the mainline churches, so that religious attendance or prayer are no longer reliable indicators of cultural and moral dispositions. Tocqueville, living in a less secular, less permissive age, could assume that "each sect worships God in its own fashion, but all preach the same morality in the name of God." That is no longer the case. The churches do not preach the same morality; some do not presume to preach any morality. Many ministers happily preside over marriage services where the pledge of "until death do us part" has been replaced by the new dispensation, "for as long as we both shall love."

One pollster speaks of an "ethics gap" between religious faith and religious practices. More to the point is the gap between religious faith and moral practices. Thus Episcopalians tend to be liberal and latitudinarian in their social attitudes as well as in their theology, whereas Evangelicals and Mormons are typically fundamentalist in theology and traditionalist in morality. (The violent crime rate in Utah, which has the largest Mormon population, is less than half that of the United States.)

The ethics gap cuts through religions and denominations. Southern and Northern Baptists differ sharply not only on such subjects as the ordination of women and homosexuals but on cultural and moral values in general. And among Southern Baptists themselves the disagreements are severe enough to have very nearly caused a schism in recent years. Some Reform Jews regard marriage with an Orthodox Jew almost as a species of intermarriage, and would actually prefer their child to marry a non-Jew who shares their values rather than an Orthodox Jew who does not. Traditionalist Catholics are at odds with modernists. Even on the subject of abortion, where one might expect agreement, the rift is significant, with little more than a third of modernist Catholics subscribing to a pro-life position. And Protestants allied with the Christian Coalition have as little in common with those in the National Council of Churches as they do with secularists or atheists; indeed, they may be better disposed to the latter because they do not contaminate the well of religion and morality.

The religious revival we are now experiencing is also – and perhaps more so – a moral revival. This is not to deny or belittle its spiritual impulse, but only to recognize its ethical character as well. (The resemblance to the Wesleyan movement in the eighteenth century, which also had a strong ethical component, is striking; even today's televised gospel meetings recall Wesley's open-air assemblies.) It is significant that the revival has not affected the mainline churches. On the contrary, as the Evangelicals have doubled in size and the Mormons have quadrupled, the mainline churches have declined by a fourth.

The revival, which has no parallel abroad, may well bewilder a foreign visitor. It is even bewildering to those Americans who have no strong religious convictions and are fearful of the intrusion, as they see it, of religion in the public sphere. It is especially disconcerting to those academics who believe religiosity to be obsolete. Peter Berger and others have long since refuted the idea that modernization necessarily implies secularization. But intellectual habits die hard in the academy, and that theory has persisted, perhaps because it is congenial to the secular disposition of most professors. Even some professors who loudly deplore the decline of civic virtue and call for a restoration of civil society do not look to religion for the recovery of virtue or to the churches for the revitalization of society.

Journalists, who are also disproportionately liberal in politics and secular in belief, are no less dismissive of religion. A front-page story in the *Washington Post* in 1993 described Evangelicals as "poor, uneducated, and easy to command." Protests from readers obliged the *Post* to retract that statement. But the media continued to report on the religious revival *de haut en bas*, as if describing the antics of some barbarian tribe.

———

This suggests a larger "ethics gap" in our society – a gap serious enough to warrant a revival of the term "two nations." Only a few years after Tocqueville completed *Democracy in America*, Disraeli, in his novel *Sybil*, described the very different society of England, an England that comprised not one but two nations.

> *Two nations; between whom there is no intercourse and no sympathy; who are as ignorant of each other's habits, thoughts, and feelings, as if they were dwellers in different zones, or inhabitants of different planets; who are formed by different breeding, are fed by a different food, are ordered by different manners, and are not governed by the same laws.*

Disraeli's two nations were "the rich and the poor." The two nations in America today are distinguished neither by money nor by class. Nor are they the two racially divided nations described by Andrew Hacker in his 1992 book, *Two Nations:*

Black and White, Separate, Hostile, Unequal. Nor are they the two nations within the black community, the elites and the underclass, identified by Henry Louis Gates, Jr., in his 1995 book, *Two Nations . . . Both Black.*

The distinctive features of our two nations are ethos and culture rather than class, race, or ethnicity. Jean Jaurès, the French socialist and member of the Chamber of Deputies early in the twentieth century, is reputed to have said: "There is more in common between two parliamentarians, one of whom is a socialist, than between two socialists, one of whom is a parliamentarian." So, an American might now say, there is more in common between two churchgoing families, one of which is working-class, than between two working-class families, only one of which is churchgoing; or between two two-parent families, one of which is black, than between two black families, only one of which has two parents. (The statistics support these assertions: Blacks and whites who grew up with two parents have low crime rates; blacks and whites who grew up in broken homes have high crime rates.)

The two-nations divide runs through race, religion, ethnicity, class, party, and sex. It is because their identity is defined primarily by moral and cultural values that many inner-city black parents send their children to Catholic schools even when they themselves are not Catholic: they want their children to have a more rigorous education in a more disciplined environment than is available in the public schools. For the same reason, some nonobservant Jews send their children to Jewish day schools rather than public or even private secular schools.

The divide makes for strange bedfellows. Some Orthodox Jews are finding, to their surprise, that they have more in common with Protestant fundamentalists and Catholic traditionalists (on such subjects as school vouchers, gay marriage, or sex education in the schools) than with their brethren in the Reform or even Conservative denominations. And the old animosity between Catholics and Protestants is giving way to a sense of common cause between traditionalists in both religions. It is not unusual to find an Orthodox rabbi, a Catholic priest, and a black Baptist preacher sharing the head table with Evangelicals at a conference of the Christian Coalition, which itself has spawned a Catholic Alliance that is committed to the same social and moral values. James Davison Hunter refers to the "pragmatic alliances being formed across faith traditions," with cultural conservatives pitted against progressives. Others speak of a shift from "ethnocultural" to "ideological" coalitions, leading to "cross-tradition alliances" of liberals against conservatives.

As religious alliances are reconstituting themselves on moral and cultural grounds, racial segregation is also breaking down. In the past, only liberal denominations were integrated. Now conservative ones are as well, with white Southern Baptist churches opening their doors to blacks, and Evangelical organizations endorsing the principle of "racial reconciliation." Political affiliations have undergone similar realignments. It was the state of the culture, not "the economy, stupid," that prompted many working-class Democrats to switch their lifelong allegiances and vote for Reagan in 1980. And the voting patterns in 1996 showed a division not between Protestants and Catholics but between traditionalists and modernists in both religions.

———

The two-nations image was surely overdramatized by Disraeli and can easily be exaggerated today. Then, as now, a large part of the population falls somewhere between those two nations. Yet that image did illuminate an essential aspect of early Victorian England. And it does help explain the peculiar, almost schizoid nature of our present condition: the sense of moral disarray on the one hand, and the visible, even dramatic evidence of a moral-*cum*-religious revival on the other. This disjunction is apparent in small matters and large – in the fact, for example, that gangsta rap and gospel rock are both among today's fastest-growing forms of music. Or that, amid all the evidence of family breakdown, we also have the "Promise Keepers," the half million men who in October 1997 assembled on the National Mall in Washington for a day of prayer and atonement, pledging themselves to Christian observance, marital fidelity, and familial responsibility. In local meetings of fifty thousand or so, they pay for the privilege of participating in demonstrations of this kind.

The moral polarization of society is most conspicuous in such hotly disputed issues as school vouchers, prayer in public schools, partial-birth abortion, pornography on the Internet, or homosexuality and adultery in the military. But it has larger ramifications, affecting beliefs, attitudes, and values on a host of subjects ranging from private morality to public policy. It is, in fact, more profoundly divisive than the class polarization that Marxists looked to as the precondition for their revolution.

———

Having been spared a class revolution, we have finally succumbed to the cultural revolution. What was a subculture or counterculture only a few decades ago is now the dominant culture. For some time, conservatives resisted acknowledging this development, convinced that "the people" were still "sound," still devoted to traditional values, and that only superficially and intermittently were they (or more often, their children) seduced by the blandishments of the counterculture. That confidence has eroded, as surely as the values themselves have. By now, it is evident that the counterculture of yesteryear is the dominant culture today. "Alternative lifestyles" that only a few decades ago were frowned upon by polite society are now not only tolerated but given equal status with traditional lifestyles. An "adversary culture" once confined to artists (and *artistes-manqués* known as "bohemians") has been democratized and popularized. Family values once taken for granted are now, if not derided as "bourgeois values," then widely ignored and violated with impunity.

Like all cultures, the dominant culture today exhibits a wide spectrum of beliefs and practices. At one end is the elite culture, as it has been called, represented by the media and academia. Statistics confirm what we all know – that the views of the media and academia are consistently more permissive and "progressive" than those of the public. Thus only a third of the public but 90 percent in the media support the right to abortion without qualification. Well over half of the public but only 5 percent of leading filmmakers say that they attend church at least once a month. More than three-quarters of the public but fewer than half in the media say that adultery is always wrong. Both adultery and promiscuity are portrayed frequently and sympathetically in films and television. The favorable portrayals of casual sex on TV outnumber the unfavorable by twenty to one.

But the elites are only a part, if a most visible and influential part, of this culture. The bulk of the people are acquiescent and passive. Even when they express conservative views on some subjects, they do not feel strongly enough to take a vigorous or consistent stand on them. They believe in God, but they believe even more in the autonomy of the individual. They say that one cannot legislate morality, but what they mean is that one should not adjudicate morality. They find it difficult to judge what is moral or immoral even for themselves, still more for others. Thus they take refuge in such circumlocutions as "Who is to say . . . ?" or "Personally, I oppose abortion, but . . ."

Most people have misgivings about "sexually active" teenagers, and with good reason; according to a recent survey, one-fifth of fifteen-year-olds and one-half of seventeen-year-olds have had sex, many on frequent occasions and with multiple partners. But the same people tend to be tolerant of sexually active college students and adults. Only one-quarter think that premarital sex is always wrong, and two-fifths, that it is not wrong at all. Almost half of parents with young children say that their primary goal is to raise a moral child, compared with just over a third who give priority to the happiness of the child, but what those parents mean by morality is not specified in the poll and probably not clear to themselves. Nearly everyone professes to believe in "family values," but the concept of the family has radically changed. It is not only sociologists who define the "postmodern family" as almost any combination of individuals, and some dismiss the very idea of "family" (in quotation marks) as having no objective meaning at all. More significant is the fact that almost three-quarters of the public reject the traditional (and until recently, the legal) concept of family as people related by blood, marriage, or adoption, in favor of the expansive notion of "a group of people who love and care for each other."

If the dominant nation expresses the values of what was once the counterculture, the "other" nation may be said to represent a counter-counterculture. Here too, one finds a spectrum of beliefs and behavior, ranging from a rigid adherence to traditional values only occasionally violated in practice, to a somewhat more lenient set of values more often violated. But even the laxer members of this other nation are more assured in their values and less diffident about expressing them than their counterparts in the dominant nation. "Who am I to say ...?" and "Personally ... but" are not in their lexicon.

At one end of the spectrum of this other nation (paralleling the cultural elite of the dominant nation) is the "Religious Right." This is the hard core of the other nation – a determined and articulate group of Evangelical Protestants. In a recent survey, 18 percent of the public identified themselves by this label. Yet even they are not homogeneous either in theology or in politics; they vary in the degree of their fundamentalism and conservatism. Forty-three percent of the public describe themselves as "born-again" Christians, but only one-third of these associate themselves with the Religious Right. The other nation, then, extends well beyond the Religious Right. It includes traditionalist Protestants, Catholics, Mormons, some Orthodox Jews (the latter a very small number proportionately), and individuals of no particular religious affiliation but of strong traditional moral convictions.

Although this other nation is an important and often vocal presence in the polity, so that neither party can ignore it with impunity, it is a minority of the population. A recent survey of the "political culture" (in which moral attitudes and issues loom large) produced a typology of six categories: the two traditional groups ("traditionalists" and "neo-traditionalists") constituting 27 percent of the population, the two liberal ones ("communitarians" and "permissivists") 46 percent, and the two intermediate, moderate ones ("pragmatists" and "conventionalists") 29 percent. The other nation is clearly outweighed numerically. As a result, it labors under the disadvantage of being perennially on the defensive. Its elite – gospel preachers, radio talk-show hosts, a few prominent columnists, and organizational leaders – cannot begin to match that of the dominant nation occupying the commanding heights of the culture: the professors who preside over a multitude of young people who have to attend their lectures, read their books, and pass their examinations; the journalists who determine what information comes to the public and with what "spin"; the television and movie producers who provide the images, models, and values that shape the popular culture; the corporate leaders who willingly produce whatever the public will buy, indeed, are ingenious in creating a market for new and ever more meretricious products.

Yet as the dominant elite becomes more audacious in defying conventional values – "pushing the envelope," as is said – it risks provoking a reaction on the part of an otherwise acquiescent public. Even those who have been long inured to such excesses may be repelled by the latest TV serial that is acclaimed as "push[ing] the limits of network television" and "stretching the acceptable" – that is, setting new standards of violence, profanity, and prurience; or by the new game on the Internet by the creators of *Sesame Street*, a game with the dual distinction of being one of the goriest yet produced and a tremendous commercial success; or by the Pulitzer-prize-winning drama celebrating not so much homosexuality as pornography and obscenity; or by the "Distinguished Professor" who flaunts her sexual relations with her students as a higher form of scholarship and pedagogy.

Some professors are beginning to complain that their students are resisting the prevailing academic fashions and are becoming conservative – career-minded, they contemptuously call it – and even religious. *The Chronicle of Higher Education* reports on a surge of religious activities on college campuses. Pollsters tell us that half of teenagers attend church, and an increasing number do so of their own accord rather than because of pressure from their parents. Young people are also becoming less enchanted with their sexual liberation. In the past few years, the number of college freshmen who believe that abortion should be legal declined from 65 percent to 56 percent, and those who approve of casual sex from 51 percent to 42 percent. This tendency cuts across class lines: 83 percent of inner-city high-school juniors and seniors, asked about the ideal age to start having sex, gave an age older than that when they themselves had first had sex.

Their elders are also reconsidering the sexual permissiveness of their own youth. More than half of those who now say that premarital sex is always wrong had themselves had sex before marriage; and a fourth of those who say that sex for a young teenager is always wrong had had sex at that young age. Twenty-five years ago, one-seventh of those in their twenties said that premarital sex was always wrong; today, one-fourth of that generation (now in their forties) believe it is always wrong. At that time, one-third of the twenty-somethings thought divorce should be more difficult to obtain; today, almost half of those in their forties (and somewhat less than half of those now in their twenties) hold that opinion.

The dominant ethos, then, is still dominant, but a reaction against it is growing – among young people who will shape the culture of the future, and among their elders who have person-

ally experienced the effects of a revolution that promised liberation and brought, all too often, grief and disaster.

———

Historians have not been notably successful in predicting the
future. They are not even, as some wit has said, very good at
predicting the past. Some observers of the religious revival
predicted the demise of religion when the Moral Majority dis-
banded in the late 1980s. They were woefully wrong. More
recently, others have predicted a new religious "Awakening"
that would transform the ethos and culture of the United States
as did the Great Awakenings of the eighteenth and nineteenth
centuries. I have more modest expectations. I think the reli-
gious-*cum*-moral revival will continue to invigorate the other
nation, without succeeding in converting the dominant nation.
It will, however, serve the vital function of keeping alive an
alternative ethos and culture – an alternative that will not necessarily have a religious character.

Those who urge us to be tolerant of "alternative lifestyles" –
and not only to be tolerant of them but to give them full credence
and legitimacy – have in mind such lifestyles as single-parent
families, gay marriages, or cohabitation and procreation without benefit of marriage. But there are other alternatives, traditional lifestyles, that are reasserting themselves within that other
nation and even beginning to be reflected in public policies.

The welfare-reform bill of 1996, for example, is not merely
an alternative way of administering welfare. It is an attempt to
promote an alternative ethos, a new attitude toward dependency and all the ills associated with it. Critics say that the
reform has not yet had a measurable effect on out-of-wedlock

births. But it does represent a significant change in public opinion, which (if the reform is sustained) will eventually be reflected in the statistics. In the meantime, it has succeeded in reducing the relief rolls and, more important, in inspiring a new appreciation for what was once derided (in some circles, is still derided) as the "bourgeois work ethic." A poll of women on welfare in New Jersey, which has a "family cap" policy denying additional benefits for new births to mothers already on the relief rolls, showed two-thirds of them judging the policy to be fair and more than four-fifths praising it for promoting responsibility; only one-half said that it hurt children, and one-third that it interfered with a woman's right to have a baby.

In education, alternatives to the dominant culture are offered by charter schools and voucher systems, which enable poor parents to do what the rich have always done: send their children to the school of their choice. Still another is the "covenant marriage" instituted by Louisiana, according to which couples forfeit their right to no-fault divorce and agree to a more binding marriage contract. Implicit in both cases is the recognition that the dominant culture will not soon be changed; the public school system is not likely to be significantly reformed in the near future, and the no-fault divorce law is not about to be repealed. But the alternatives are important not only because they make available other modes of education and marriage, but also because these modes have been legitimized and institutionalized by the state.

Some alternatives do not require the intervention of the state; they require only that the state forbear from intervening. Private schools, and especially religious schools, have long been available but are now far more numerous than they have ever been, in the suburbs as well as the inner cities, and appealing to all classes and races. (Jewish day schools now cut across denominational lines; the largest number are still Orthodox, but they are being joined by nondenominational ones that include adherents of the Conservative and even Reform movements.)

A more radical alternative is homeschooling; it is estimated that a million or more children are now being educated at home. This movement has advanced to the point where a new two-year college is being planned especially for homeschoolers. Analogous to homeschooling is the "TV-free" home. At a time when television is becoming increasingly intrusive and aggressive, more and more parents are making the deliberate decision not to have television in their homes, Two million households, most of them with children, now practice this kind of "cultural abstinence" – yet another means by which the other nation voluntarily opts out of the dominant culture.

This other nation, then, is not a cure for the diseases incident to a democratic society, but it is a way of containing and mitigating those diseases. Moreover, it does so in an eminently democratic fashion, consistent with the original Federalists who assumed that virtue – and religion of sorts, if only of the deist sort – was a necessary attribute of the citizens of a large republic, although not a direct or primary responsibility of the government. The other nation, reconciled to its minority status in what is now a very large and varied republic indeed, has no ambitions to impose its values upon others; it only seeks to promote and protect those values for itself. It does not want to alter the constitutional arrangements separating church and state, but only resists the efforts of the courts to go beyond that separation by creating a hostile environment for religion as such. Nor does it desire a more active role for government than that which has been traditional in America until very recently, as exemplified in the principle of community standards applied to pornography. More often than not, restoring traditional practices means favoring a less intrusive government (as in the matter of sex education).

The other nation is self-selecting and self-sustaining. It is not, however, entirely self-sufficient. Even within this other nation, there is no guarantee of immunity from the diseases afflicting society; the dominant culture is too pervasive and powerful. Nor would it be desirable to immunize this other nation entirely, even if that were possible. The dominant culture has too much of value to warrant the kind of segregation or quarantine that would require. Opting out of the culture is hardly an ideal solution. School vouchers and homeschooling are defensive measures, a last resort against a seriously flawed public school system that was once the pride of our democracy. So, too, gated and segregated communities are understandable but unfortunate expediencies in a country that values openness and mobility. The parents of TV-deprived children have good reason to worry about the "forbidden fruit" syndrome. And even covenant marriages have unwitting side effects. The requirement of premarital counseling, like prenuptial contracts, may induce a premature sense of doubt and uncertainty where there should be confidence and security. And any alternative form of marriage makes the conventional one seem even more precarious, an open invitation to divorce.

TV "abstainers" have been called "a band of internal exiles." It would be regrettable if the other nation were reduced to that lowly status. One can only hope that eventually the diseases will run their course, and the nations will, more or less, reunite.

This is, after all, what happened in Disraeli's time, when industrialism and education gradually diminished the gap between
rich and poor, so that by the end of the nineteenth century they
had become mere classes rather than distinct nations. It is not
unreasonable to suppose that our own two nations will evolve
in the same fashion. And it is very much the desire of the other
nation that this happen. A 1996 survey conducted by the Roper
Organization found that the supporters of the Christian Right
were "among the most unwavering in their commitment to the
American political system." Forty-eight percent scored high in
"respect for the political institutions in America," compared
with one-third of the general population; 71 percent took pride
in living "under our political system," compared with 61 percent of the whole; 68 percent felt strongly that "our system of
government is the best possible system," compared with 53
percent of the whole; and 85 percent said they "support our
system of government," compared with 65 percent of the
whole. They were disaffected, to be sure, with the condition of
the political culture, but entirely loyal to America as a country,
a creed, and a polity – a single nation.

The example of Victorian England emboldens me to make
another prediction. There too the religious revival, inspired by
the Methodists and Evangelicals, had from its inception a
strong moral impulse. And there, in the course of the nineteenth century, the moral part of that revival gradually over-
shadowed the religious part, so that by the end of the century,
the moral-reformation movement counted among its followers
not only Methodists and Evangelicals but also High Church

Anglicans, Catholics, dissenters of every denomination, and, not least, a good body of secularists. This is already becoming evident in the United States. As religious groups begin to feel more self-confident and less beleaguered, they will shed some of their sectarianism and intransigence. Witness, for example, the shift in tactics from a constitutional amendment reversing *Roe v. Wade* to a policy designed to chip away at abortion incrementally. Religious groups will also become more hospitable to those secularists who share their values. Indeed, this was anticipated in the late 1970s when the Christian Right associated itself with the secular New Right. It was then that Jerry Falwell, inaugurating what he optimistically called the Moral Majority, defined it as including "fundamentalists, Protestants, Roman Catholics, Jews, Mormons, and persons of no particular religious convictions at all who believe in the moral principles we espouse."

It is in this latitudinarian sense that the Moral Majority might become just that – a majority of Americans of all religious creeds, and of none, sharing a common ethos. By then, too, the religious element may have become so attenuated that historians will have to remind their contemporaries (as we have been reminded in our own time) that they are living off the religious capital of a previous generation, and that this capital is being perilously depleted. Society may then find itself caught up in yet another cycle of demoralization and remoralization, including, perhaps, another Great Awakening.

But such prophecies take us far into the future. For the moment, let us be content with the knowledge that the two nations can live together in the present (as they did in early Victorian England) with some degree of tension and dissension but without civil strife or anarchy. And (recalling the example of late Victorian England) we may even look forward to something like a reconciliation of the two nations – at the very least, to an abatement of the diseases incident to democratic society.

1998

CHAPTER SIXTEEN

Compassionate Conservatism: 18th-Century England and 21st-Century America

———————•‖‖‖•———————

DEFEAT, LIKE DEATH, concentrates the mind wonderfully. It also liberates the mind. People venture to think the unthinkable, or at least the impermissible. A new generation of conservatives may be moved to reconsider some ideas that have fallen into disuse or even disrepute. Compassion is one such idea.

Shortly after the 2012 election, Paul Ryan, addressing the Kemp Foundation, took the measure of the situation in which conservatives found themselves. In the course of his remarks, he uttered the word "compassion" or "compassionate" at least five times – in a favorable sense. This is all the more striking because American conservatives have not always been comfortable with that word, regarding it as a vapid sentimentalism that has no place in politics, let alone economics. President Bush's adoption of a policy of "compassionate conservatism" in his first term confirmed them in that suspicion, for the policy soon degenerated into what conservatives themselves derided as a "politics of compassion," consisting of yet another round of programs conceived and financed by the government and farmed out to "faith-based" (a euphemism for "religious") institutions. This was all too reminiscent of the "Great Society" (with "society" a euphemism for "state") inaugurated by President Johnson, which set in motion the vast expansion of the welfare state. (The latter term has now fallen into disuse, as the present entitlement system goes well beyond the "welfare" designed for the relief of poverty.)

Anticipating the objection that might be made to that term, Ryan reminded us that we should measure compassion not by how much we spend, and certainly not by how much the government spends or how many programs it creates, but by how many people we help. Yet his own endorsement of compassion is reassuring. It is because of his impeccable conservative credentials that we may dare revive the word, and with it a new conservatism, a remoralized conservatism, one might say. Conservatives have always maintained that conservative ideas – of government, the economy, society, the family – are based on sound moral principles. But the case has been made almost as an afterthought. Ryan proposed to bring it to the forefront. "We have a compassionate vision based on ideas that work," he told us. "But sometimes we don't do a good job of laying out that vision." Compassion – the word and the idea – may help give shape and substance to that vision.

———

It may also be helpful to put that word and idea in historical perspective, to recall its lineage and something of its history, most pertinently in modern times. "To compassionate, i.e., to join with in passion," the Earl of Shaftesbury wrote early in the eighteenth century, "... to commiserate, i.e., to join with in misery ... this in one order of life is right and good; nothing more harmonious; and to be without this, or not to feel this, is unnatural, horrid, immane [inhuman]." Half a century later, Adam Smith, in *The Theory of Moral Sentiments*, distinguished between sympathy and compassion: sympathy being the "fellow-feeling" of all men for each other, compassion the "fellow-feeling" for the sorrow of others. "Sympathy" and "compassion," "moral sense" and "moral sentiments," "social affections" and "social virtues" – these are the terms that dominated social and philosophical discourse and gave a unique character to the British Enlightenment.

This is also the moral philosophy that distinguishes Smith's political economy from the prevailing mercantilist doctrine. *The Wealth of Nations* moralizes the economy even as it liberalizes and liberates it from the government and the state. So, too, the people are moralized. The working classes, including the very poor, are said to share a common human nature with their employers and social superiors. They are driven by the same instinct, "the propensity to truck, barter, and exchange"; they have the same motive, to "better themselves"; and they enjoy the same benefits of a thriving economy, a "universal opulence which extends itself to the lowest ranks of the people." Indeed, the difference between "a philosopher and a common street porter," Smith declares, comes "not so much from nature, as from habit, custom, and education."

Smith was a professor of moral philosophy before he became a political economist, so the rhetoric of morality came naturally to him. Conservatives of a libertarian bent are discomfited by his frequent denunciations – not in *The Theory of Moral Sentiments*, where one might expect them, but in *The Wealth of Nations* – of merchants and manufacturers who espouse "the vile maxim, 'all for themselves, and nothing for other people,'" and who are prone to "impertinent jealousy," "mean rapacity," "malignant expedients," "sneaking arts," "interesting sophistry," and "interested falsehood."

The compassion that Smith found in human nature exhibited itself not only in individual acts of charity but in a proliferation of "societies" (Tocqueville was to call them "associations") to alleviate every kind of affliction and misfortune. Contemplating those societies – for abandoned infants, abused children, fallen women, maimed seamen, the deaf, dumb, blind, crippled, and insane – the reformer Hannah More characterized her period (not entirely in praise) as the "Age of Benevolence." The early Victorians, inspired by the Evangelicals, added the slave trade and child labor to that list. Later still, Josephine Butler, championing the cause of prostitutes, described "the awful abundance of compassion which makes me fierce." Beatrice Webb summed up the "time-spirit" of these late Victorians as the "Religion of Humanity" – a term coined by the positivists, for whom humanitarianism (or "fellow-feeling," as Smith would have said) was a surrogate for religion itself. This new religion, she explained, for positivists and reformers like herself, had a double aspect, uniting religion and science in the service of humanity.

It was in this spirit that yet another society, the Charity Organisation Society, was formed in 1869. Its purpose was to rationalize ("scientize," so to speak) the "abundance of compassion" exhibited in the philanthropic societies – seven hundred in London alone. In three years there were three dozen district committees, and by the end of the 1870s the COS was the premier charitable organization in London and a model for others in England and America. Charles Loch, its longtime secretary, commented on the apparent paradox in the title, "charity" being "free, fervent, impulsive," and "organization" implying "order, method, . . . self-restraint." The COS sought to make charity more effective by eliminating duplication and encouraging new methods for the identification and supervision of the recipients of charity. Like the other societies, it was a private enterprise, founded, funded, directed, and staffed without any government contribution or involvement (without even the tax-code incentive that modern philanthropies enjoy). And like them, it was intended to help individuals and families help themselves. "Charity," Loch declared, "is a social regenerator. We have to use Charity to create the power of self-help."

The "self" in "self-help" applied as much to the family as to the individual. It was for the sake of the family that other philanthropists addressed themselves to the problem of housing. Bad housing, they claimed, was even more detrimental to the poor than unemployment, because the home was the heart and hearth of the family, and the family was crucial to the development of character. Earlier in the century another Lord Shaftesbury had founded the Society for Improving the Condition of the Labouring Classes, which had as one of its main functions the building and renovating of houses for the poor. Other societies followed suit, constructing "model dwellings" where tenants were required to pay a modest rent.

Octavia Hill, one of the founding members of the Charity Organisation Society, took this as her main cause, buying houses that she renovated and managed, with a staff of "rent collectors" doubling as social workers. Like a latter-day psychoanalyst justifying the hourly fee as a token of the patient's earnestness, she regarded the prompt payment of rent as an earnest of the tenant's good faith and good conduct. Notably hardheaded in this respect, she was also sensitive to the spiritual and aesthetic needs of her tenants. Criticizing the municipally built model dwellings for not being sufficiently "model," she paid as much attention to the landscaping as to the interiors of her houses. "The poor of London," she reminded reformers, "need joy and beauty in their lives."

Another notable institution, the Salvation Army, founded by the Methodist "Christian Mission," was an amalgam not of religion and science, but the equally improbable combination of religion and the military. It declared itself an "army" complete with "corps" (local societies), "forts" (shelters), "soldiers" (members), and "officers" (missionaries). On the theory that spiritual salvation required a prior moral reformation, and that in turn a material reformation, it provided the poor not only with such uplifting activities as revivalist meetings, singings, and entertainment, but also with material comforts: shelters for the homeless, homes for "fallen women," prison-gate "brigades" to help released convicts, and food depots for the needy. By the end of the century it had taken on a still more ambitious project, the founding of "colonies" – city, farm, and overseas colonies – each to be a "self-helping and self-sustaining" community.

Toynbee Hall catered to a different constituency, not the very poor or indigent but the working classes as a whole. It is perhaps not coincidental that Toynbee Hall, the first settlement house in London, was established at the same time as the passage of the Reform Act of 1884, which enfranchised most of the working classes. Toynbee Hall (named in honor of Arnold Toynbee, the economic historian and uncle of the more famous historian) was meant to bridge the gap between the "two nations" by uniting them in a common "citizenship" – a moral as well as political citizenship. The rich would fulfill their civic responsibilities by instructing and catering to the poor, and the poor by acquiring the education and culture that enabled them to be active and worthy citizens. The settlement houses, in working-class neighborhoods, were residences not for the poor but for those who ministered to them, university graduates mainly from Oxford who paid for their lodging and food, and lived there for several months or even years. Neighboring workers would meet there for classes, lectures, discussions, concerts, exhibits, or whatever else might be edifying and elevating, in an atmosphere that was itself edifying and elevating. Toynbee Hall was deliberately constructed to resemble an Oxford college. By the end of the century there were thirty such houses, over half of them in London.

These were only the more conspicuous manifestations of the "abundance of compassion" testified to by Josephine Butler and the scores of philanthropists who dedicated their entire lives to charitable enterprises of one sort or another. They were not people of great fortune. Octavia Hill had to borrow money from her good friend John Ruskin for the purchase of her first three houses, and the college graduates in Toynbee Hall paid for the privilege of serving the community. In this respect, late Victorian England was the very model of a civil society. The societies and institutions were privately organized and funded, focused on specific causes, and supervised to make sure that the efforts produced the desired results. They all relied, for their moral as well as financial support, upon the other resources of civil society – individuals, families, friends, and religious missions of all denominations. And they all shared a common ethos. As help was given as a charity, not a tax, so it was received as a gift, not an entitlement.

That ethos, and the civil society that sustained it, began to be challenged early in the following century by the enactment of two critical pieces of legislation: old age and unemployment insurance. It is ironic to find Beatrice Webb, now better known as a founder of English socialism, opposing those acts because they gave people money allowances unconditionally, with no return expected in the form of better conduct or an attempt to seek or retain work. It is even more ironic to find Winston Churchill, then a Liberal, defending them on the grounds that social policy should not be grounded in moral criteria. "I do not like mixing up moralities and mathematics," he explained. Three decades later, the Beveridge Report of 1942 heralded the welfare state as the next "British revolution." That revolution was carried out after the war with a series of acts, including the National Health Service Act, that transferred many of the duties and responsibilities of civil society to the welfare state.

Half a century later, when the welfare state had been transformed into something like an entitlement state, David Cameron adopted President Bush's motto of "compassionate conservatism." He later reaffirmed the principle: "It's not enough to know our ideas are right. We've got to explain why they are compassionate too." Unfortunately, the British version of compassionate conservatism, intended to strengthen civil society by making it the instrument for the public expression of compassion, has the opposite effect. The programs that go under that label are more often initiated ("encouraged," as is said), supervised, and even partly subsidized by the government.

In this country, a new generation of conservatives, confronting similar problems, may well look to some old sages for inspiration – to Adam Smith most notably, not only for his economic principles but also for the moral vision that informed them. One might even quote Smith against Churchill, reminding him that social policies, and economic policies as well, are necessarily, for good or bad, grounded in moral criteria. On the other hand, a conservative might well agree with Churchill that those early measures of social legislation, and some later ones as well, were both warranted and effective. One can also look to American history for the assurance that civil society is not an abstract or ideal concept but very much a reality, a vehicle for reform as well as for the preservation of tradition – the "status quo," as is said invidiously.

Above all, what conservatives can do is to recapture compassion from the liberals, desentimentalizing it while reaffirming it. Properly understood, compassion is a preeminently conservative virtue. It dignifies the individual, the donor of charity as well as the recipient; it thrives in a free and sound economy where the individual can "better himself"; it nurtures a spirit of independence rather than fostering the dependency that is too often the result of misguided entitlements; and it finds expression and fulfillment in civil society more often than in government.

This is not to deny the validity or utility of safety nets and entitlements in principle, but only to define and limit them in practice. Nor is it to deny any role to government, but only, again, to define that role more precisely and to limit it more severely. Leo Strauss once wrote, in another context: "A conservative, I take it, is a man who despises vulgarity; but the argument which is concerned exclusively with calculations of success, and is based on blindness to the nobility of the effort, is vulgar." If only on that ground – the nobility of the effort – compassion should endear itself to the conservative.

2013

CHAPTER SEVENTEEN

Our Fourth of July and the Queen's Diamond Jubilee

I T WAS PERHAPS inevitable that our Fourth of July celebrations might have seemed anticlimactic after the four-day festivities that marked Queen Elizabeth's Diamond Jubilee in June 2012, celebrating her sixty years on the throne. Fireworks, however spectacular, cannot compare to the thousand-boat flotilla on the Thames, with great throngs of riverside spectators shivering and soaking in torrential rain, or to the horse-drawn carriage procession from Westminster Hall to Buckingham Palace, the Queen regally bedecked and costumed, cheered by crowds lining the streets. A panorama worthy of Hollywood, it was reported, televised, and enthusiastically hailed throughout the world, with the Queen as the star of the show, a worthy successor to that other Good Queen Bess whose name she bears.

On second thought, it is the Jubilee that, to an American at least, may have been anticlimactic, a display of mere "virtual reality," while the Fourth of July commemorates a truly momentous event. In liberating us from that monarchy, the Declaration of Independence delivered a devastating blow to the very idea of monarchy, preparing the way for a republic that was not only a new form of government but also a new social order. Almost in that instant, the New World made the old monarchical world appear archaic and obsolete. It is as if we had ushered in modernity itself. Now, in the twenty-first century, with modernity so far advanced that it threatens to be superseded by something called postmodernity, we have been regaled with a "reality show" glorifying an institution that seems to defy modernity, flaunting a monarch who is only the figurehead of a commonwealth that is a mere remnant of the British Empire.

Today, when Americans find the very word "lady" suspect, we are shown the British paying homage not only to Ladies (officially titled and capitalized), but also to princesses, and of course the Queen. While we have discarded, in the name of equality, such courtesies as men opening doors for women, we are regaled with images of commoners, however exalted in other respects, curtsying to the Queen, and princesses of lesser title curtsying to princesses of blood. Indeed, those "commoners" (the word itself is invidious to an American ear) are not citizens but subjects of the Crown. And these social amenities do not begin to take into account the more serious anomalies, such as the cost of the royal households in a period of economic crisis and austerity. To an American, the monarchy is surely Britain's "peculiar institution," as slavery was ours. And the Jubilee, celebrating the monarchy, is surely a triumph of nostalgia over reality.

Or perhaps not. In paying tribute to the Queen – the grace and dignity with which she carries out her ceremonial duties – the British are testifying to her real public function, which is to reassert, in the face of all evidence to the contrary, the unity, continuity, and vitality of the polity as well as society. This is why in recent times there has been no whiff of the abolitionism – the abolition of the monarchy rather than of slavery – that was a recurrent theme in earlier British history. A letter to the London *Times* took a reporter to task for invoking the good behavior of the Queen as an argument in support of the monarchy. This is irrelevant, the correspondent protested: "To approve of the Queen because she is 'good at the job' rather suggests republican sympathies," implying that a Queen who was less "good at the job" would warrant the abolition of the monarchy. The same objection might be made to an article in the *Wall Street Journal* that explained why Americans should "hail the Queen." "Slyly witty and supremely dutiful, she is the glue holding together a modern, multicultural Commonwealth" – as if it were the wit and dutifulness that provided the glue, rather than the sentiments attached to the monarchy itself. Almost in passing, the article cited the Victorian writer about the monarchy who warned the English: "We must not let daylight in upon magic."

In fact, it was that eminent Victorian, Walter Bagehot, who let daylight in by exposing the magical function of the monarchy. Bagehot's *The English Constitution* is outmoded in some respects; it was written in the two years before the passage of the 1867 Reform Act, which was a major advance toward democracy. But it is still a remarkably perceptive analysis of the monarchy – of the monarchy then and, more provocatively, of the monarchy now, in the most democratic and modern of times.

Any successful constitution, Bagehot maintains, consists of two essential parts: "First, those which excite and preserve the reverence of the population – the *dignified* parts, if I may so call them; and next, the *efficient* parts – those by which it, in fact, works and rules" (italics in the original). Practical men might like to do away with the first. They look only to means and results, and in that equation the dignified parts appear to be useless. But even as a practical matter, that is mistaken, for it is the dignified parts that give "force" to government and "attract its motive power"; the efficient parts only utilize that force and employ that power. The dignified parts "raise the army, though they do not win the battle." But without the army, there would be no battle.

These remarks appear early in the book, in the chapter on the cabinet, as if to remind the reader that even that most efficient part of the government is of secondary importance to the monarchy, the dignified part. The following chapter on the monarchy (which, appropriately, is twice as long as that on the cabinet) opens unambiguously: "The use of the Queen, in a dignified capacity, is incalculable. Without her in England, the present English government would fail and pass away." The "best reason" for the strength of the monarchy is that it is an "intelligible government." The figure of the monarch, in the person of the Queen, is easily seen and understood, capturing the imagination and engaging the feelings of the people. She is not only the visible head of the government, she is also the visible head of society, of religion, and of morality, thus enlisting those formidable institutions in support of the government. "Lastly," and "far the greatest" reason for the strength of a monarchy, is that "it acts as a disguise. It enables our real rulers to change without heedless people knowing it."

That last and "greatest" reason might seem to be at odds with the first, "best" reason, the "intelligible government," which now appears to be a government in "disguise." In fact, the two are of a piece. It is precisely because the monarchy is visible and therefore intelligible that it can so successfully disguise the changes going on in the efficient parts of the government. The monarchy thus assures the unity and continuity of government even as cabinet ministers and members of Parliament, parties and policies, issues and controversies come and go.

A modern reader, particularly an American reader, might well be offended by the image of a people so unintelligent as to require the spuriously "intelligible" symbol of the monarchy; a "heedless people" incapable of understanding the ideas or activities of their "real rulers"; the "masses" who are "not fit for elective government." In defense of Bagehot, one might say that he did respect the intelligence – that is, the common sense – of the people in their common lives and affairs. What he did not respect is their ability to cope with the intricacies and complexities of politics. Thus, he opposed the extension of the suffrage in England to give the people an active role in government. And he was hostile to the American republic, which presumed to do just that. Indeed, much of *The English Constitution* is devoted to a contrast between the American and the English systems.

It is curious that nowhere does Bagehot comment on the title of his book. "English" rather than "British" did not require comment because it was the common usage at the time. "Constitution" did, particularly in the capitalized form in which it appears throughout the book. The sense in which Bagehot uses the term is, of course, its lowercase, generic one, referring to the body of common law and institutions that had governed England for centuries. But after the passage of the American Constitution (properly capitalized), which was debated and formally promulgated as a single document setting forth the binding articles of government, the contrast with the informal British constitution was all the more pronounced. Had Bagehot reflected upon the word itself, he might have said that the very act of writing a constitution, let alone a republican constitution, is evidence of a faulty government, artificial, contrived, and therefore unsound. Instead, his critique of the American

Constitution focuses on the separation of powers, which critically impairs the efficient part of government, and on the lack of any dignified part, a more fatal flaw in his view.

The Americans, Bagehot observes, could not have become monarchical, even if the Constitutional Convention had so desired, because the people lack "the mystic allegiance, the religious reverence, which are essential to a true monarchy." Elsewhere, however, describing the clumsy technicalities and "absurd fictions" invoked to amend the U.S. Constitution, he likens the Americans to "trustees carrying out a misdrawn will," hampered "by the old words of an old testament." The Constitution as an "old testament" – surely this suggests something like a mystic or religious reverence, not unlike that characterizing a monarchy.

Rebutting Bagehot, an American might defend the separation of powers as making for a government at least as efficient as the English, and might find in the Constitution itself a quality that has all the dignity, even the reverence, he attributes to the monarchy. Indeed, an American might venture to suggest that the Constitution – not one part of it but the whole of it – is a more reliable source of dignity and reverence than the monarchy, precisely because it is not dependent upon the personal character of a monarch. Not all English monarchs, after all, have displayed the dignity or warranted the reverence of the present Queen. Americans recall all too well the less-than-admirable monarch who presided over England to such ill effect at the time of the revolution.

Bagehot has only two passing references to George Washington, the president who deliberately refused to assume, in his person or public role, anything suggestive of a monarch.

Instead, in his Farewell Address, Washington took the occasion to pay tribute to the Constitution. The Constitution, he reminded his "Friends and Fellow Citizens," must be obeyed by all because it is "sacredly obligatory upon all" – the "sacred" going beyond the merely "dignified." Almost half a century later, the young Abraham Lincoln, speaking to a young men's society in Springfield, Illinois, on the subject of "the perpetuation of our political institutions," echoed that sentiment: "Let reverence for the laws . . . become the *political* religion. . . . Let those materials [founded in reason] be molded into *general intelligence, sound morality* and, in particular, *a reverence for the constitution and laws*" (italics in the original). Again, "reverence," not for a person but for a constitution that transcends persons, as it also transcends parties, politics, and all the other divisive tendencies that afflict government.

Concluding the famous *Federalist* no. 10, James Madison beseeched his countrymen to create in the Union "a Republican remedy for the diseases most incident to Republican Government." The Constitution itself is part of that remedy. It has to be interpreted by the Supreme Court, but the justices of the Court, whatever their private views, have to defend their rulings by appealing to the Constitution. This is their final authority, their "old testament," as it is for the American polity as a whole.

It is this testament that we celebrate on the Fourth of July. Our festivities might lack the drama and pageantry of the Queen's Jubilee; after all, they occur annually and do not have to await a sixtieth anniversary. But they are every bit as jubilant, and deservedly so, for they pay tribute to a republic presided over by a constitution worthy of the dignity – and, yes, reverence – we have bestowed upon it.

2012

CHAPTER EIGHTEEN

Victorian Values,
Jewish Values

━━━━━━━━━■ ▪▪▪▪▪ ■━━━━━━━━━

I N H E R C A M P A I G N for reelection, replying to a television
interviewer who observed rather derisively that she seemed
to be approving of "Victorian values," Margaret Thatcher
enthusiastically agreed: "Oh exactly. Very much so. Those
were the values when our country became great." Quite sud-
denly, "Victorian values" seized the headlines and became an
election issue.

To Mrs. Thatcher those values were self-evident. (She preferred to call them "virtues," but the more modish word prevailed.) How could one not approve of hard work, diligence,
thrift, responsibility, civility, devotion to family, respect for law
and order – all those good old virtues? A remarkable number
of people thought otherwise. Neil Kinnock, the leader of the
opposition, declared that those were the inhuman, selfish,
materialistic values that Dickens had so memorably portrayed
in *Oliver Twist* and *Hard Times* – the values of an England
where women and children labored in cotton mills and mines
while the rich wallowed in luxury and preached the gospel of
hard work. Church leaders quoted texts from the New Testa-

ment designed to prove that the Victorian values were not Christian values. Editorial writers protested against the confusion of religious and secular values – this in a country that has an official state church. Journalists cited unemployment statistics suggesting that hard work was irrelevant if there was no work available. Prince Charles toured inner-city areas and intimated that self-help was not helping very much. Literary critics objected that Victorianism was a species of sanctimonious piety and hypocritical morality. Historians pointed out that the Victorian values were not uniquely Victorian; they were Christian values, or Puritan values, or Methodist values, or bourgeois values, and in any case, no one, ever, and least of all the Victorians, observed them.

After my own essays on the Victorians were mentioned in newspaper editorials and columns, I received moving letters from people nostalgically recalling their own Victorian parents and grandparents. When I was asked by an adviser to Mrs. Thatcher to participate in a conference on Victorian values – this only a few weeks before the general election – it occurred to me that perhaps all this was a distraction from more urgent issues and that the subject would die once the election was safely over. In fact, the controversy continues, thanks to the prime minister herself, who has returned to the subject again and again, declaring it to be at the heart of her program.

It is a curious and rare phenomenon: a prime minister, having achieved significant economic and political goals in her preceding terms of office, enters her third term determined to consolidate those achievements by rooting them in the moral principles and practices which, she firmly believes, can alone sustain them. She has made morality the issue not for rhetorical effect or partisan advantage but as a matter of policy and conviction. She is not content to cut taxes, privatize industry, encourage home ownership, stimulate trade, and otherwise promote a free and prosperous economy. She feels it necessary to legitimize and, so to speak, moralize that agenda, to show that it is not only practical and expedient but also right and proper.

———

Capitalism has always required moral legitimization but has not always received it, certainly not from politicians in high places. It did not even always receive it in Victorian England, before socialism usurped the moral high ground by claiming a monopoly of social justice and compassion. Even then the critics of capitalism – Cobbett and Carlyle, Ruskin and Morris – were often more articulate and passionate than the defenders. What the Victorians did have, however, was an ethos – a generally accepted (although not always observed) code of behavior – that was congenial to capitalism and that implicitly sanctioned and validated it.

The historian who denies that there was such a code by citing all the deviations from it is surely missing the most elementary fact about morality, which is that it can remain a reality even when it is violated in practice. Hypocrisy, La Rochefoucauld reminds us, is "the homage that vice pays to virtue." The Victorians, who went to such efforts to conceal their sexual "irregularities," as they delicately put it – or, when concealment was not possible, sought to domesticate them, to give them the appearance of propriety – were surely testifying to the power of a code that continued to bind them even as they bent it to meet their special circumstances. One thinks of George Eliot, whose nonmarriage to George Lewes (because he could not be divorced from his wife) was as domestic and conventional an arrangement as any legal marriage. They did not flaunt their

irregular relationship; on the contrary, they tried desperately
to regularize it. In the true meaning of that much-abused
expression, the code was "more honored in the breach than
the observance."

And so too with the other values (as they are now called)
that Mrs. Thatcher attributed to the Victorians – work, thrift,
prudence, temperance, above all self-reliance and personal
responsibility. Of course these were not uniquely Victorian
values. In her address to the General Assembly of the Church
of Scotland in May 1988, Mrs. Thatcher described them as
"Judaic-Christian" values, and elsewhere she associated them
with John Wesley, the eighteenth-century founder of Method-
ism. But it was in the nineteenth century that they acquired a
special urgency. When the social and moral order (and to a
lesser extent the political order) was threatened by the acceler-
ated pace of industrialism and capitalism, these values helped
stabilize, legitimize, and "moralize" that order.

There was perhaps no virtue more often invoked, more idealized and revered by the Victorians, than work. "Work is worship," Carlyle declared. "All true work is sacred; in all true
work ... there is something of divineness.... No man has
worked, or can work, except religiously; not even the poor day-
laborer, the weaver of your coat, the sewer of your shoes." And
not even, Carlyle continued, the industrialist and capitalist, the
"working aristocracy" and "captains of industry," who were
"virtually the captains of the world; if there be no nobleness in
them, there will never be an aristocracy more." Carlyle, as
usual, was being melodramatic; but he was also, as usual,
expressing a sentiment that was widely held – by radicals and
conservatives, by workers and capitalists. He knew, as everyone did, that there were idlers among the rich – "master un-
workers," he called them – as well as among the poor: the

habitual vagrants, beggars, and paupers whom contemporaries spoke of as the "undeserving poor." But these were seen as excrescences, deformities. They did not define the prevailing ethos; they defined the deviations from it, the abnormal rather than the norm.

———

Some historians do not deny the prominence of work in the Victorian ethic but deny the legitimacy of the ethic itself. There is a theory popular among radical historians because it accounts for a variety of phenomena that do not lend themselves to conventional Marxist interpretations; this is the "social-control thesis." According to this thesis, the "work ethic" and all the values associated with it – thrift, prudence, diligence, punctuality, self-discipline, self-reliance – were "middle-class" or "bourgeois" values, foisted upon the workers in order to turn them into productive members of the labor force and docile members of society.

The implications of the social-control thesis are rarely confronted by these historians. If these were middle-class values, alien to the working class, what were the values that were presumably indigenous to the working class? Were the workers, by nature or preference, indolent rather than industrious, profligate rather than frugal, drunk rather than sober, promiscuous rather than faithful, dependent rather than independent? And why did the working class betray its own values to embrace those of its enemy – values designed to exploit and subjugate it?

The familiar Marxist explanation is that the working class was the victim of "false consciousness." Just as it did not (still does not) always understand its true interests – hence the absence of a proletarian revolution – so it did not understand its own values. Unwittingly it adopted the values of the ruling class, of the dominant, "hegemonic" culture, the bourgeois culture. The difficulty with this explanation is that it is not very flattering to the working class.

It must be remembered that the social-control thesis and the theory of false consciousness are advanced not by reactionary historians seeking to denigrate the working class, but by radical historians sympathetic to it – historians like E. P. Thompson who want to rescue the poor and the oppressed from "the enormous condescension of posterity." But who is guilty of this condescension? Is it the so-called bourgeois historian who attributes to the working class the values professed by the rest of society and which he himself holds dear? Or the radical historian who assigns to the working class a distinctive set of values that he does not define, and that he himself does not share because he is not of that class? Is it more condescending to credit workers with a true knowledge of their values and interests, or to portray them as ignorant of their own values and interests, as the deluded, unhappy victims of "false consciousness"?

And who is more faithful to the historical reality: the historian who requires a theory of false consciousness to account for the inconvenient fact that most Victorian workers (like most workers today) did seem to share those supposedly middle-class values? Or the historian who recognizes and respects that fact – who knows, moreover, that it was not only the "labor aristocracy," as is sometimes claimed, who shared those values but many less-skilled workers as well, even if they less often realized them in practice? The memoirs of the most militant and radical workers, the Chartists, provide poignant testimony to their efforts to be temperate and thrifty – "respectable," as they said. That much-maligned word, "respectability," was at the heart of the Victorian ethos, the ethos of the working class

as much as of the middle class. Indeed, the central tenet of
Chartism, universal suffrage, was based on the claim to respectability, for political equality presupposed moral equality –
which is to say, respectability.

Radical historians are contemptuous of those eminent Victorians who, they say, patronized the poor by trying to make
them respectable: housing reformers who provided apartments
at low rent but insisted upon the prompt payment of rent; sanitary reformers who installed sewage and running water and
preached the virtues of cleanliness; educational reformers who
passed a public-education act to promote literacy; settlement-
house workers who gave adult-education courses that would
be the equivalent of an American college degree today; social
workers who distributed charity while dispensing lessons in
domestic economy; philanthropists who organized and subsidized societies for the relief of every variety of affliction and
misfortune, all acting on the assumption that the poor had only
to be helped to help themselves, that the poor wanted for
themselves the same things that the reformers wanted for them.

The reformers may have been unrealistic in their actions,
intentions, and expectations. But are they to be condemned for
"imposing" upon the poor the values they imposed on their
own families? Were they patronizing or condescending when
they assumed that the poor had the ability and the will to act
upon those values? Were they small-minded or mean-spirited
when they upheld a single standard of values for all classes
rather than the double standard that had prevailed for so long –
a double standard implicit in the social-control thesis? Far
from keeping the working class in a condition of inferiority
and subservience, that single standard was an invitation to economic improvement and social mobility. It implied that there
were not "two nations" but one, united by a single ethos, a

common morality. Whatever class differences there were, and they were considerable, they were just that: class differences, economic and social differences, not fundamental moral differences, not differences of character or nature or spirit.

———

There is, as it happens, a fascinating document, written a century ago, testifying to the values of one group of Victorian workers. If that group is not typical of all workers, the document itself is typical in revealing the values of an eminently Victorian reformer and commentator. The author of the document, I must confess, is not one of my favorite eminent Victorians.

Beatrice Webb was not, in fact, so much a reformer as a "social engineer," exhibiting all the disagreeable traits of that species: she was officious, presumptuous, humorless, ruthless. Yet she produced some memorable works, one of them written before she became Mrs. Webb – that is, before she married Sidney Webb and joined the Fabian Society. She was Beatrice Potter then, serving her "apprenticeship," as she called it, in the craft of social research by helping Charles Booth prepare his *Life and Labour of the People of London.* The first volume of that mammoth survey, published in 1889, contains a fascinating chapter by Beatrice Webb (I shall call her by that familiar name although she was not yet married) on the Jewish community in the East End of London.

Some historians have accused Beatrice Webb of being antisemitic. (It has also been said that she herself was, or believed herself to be, one-quarter Jewish, but this is highly speculative.) I have never seen persuasive evidence of antisemitism on her part, although later in life she was certainly anti-Zionist, as so many socialists were, including her husband. In any case,

her essay on the Jewish community in East London is anything
but antisemitic. Written at a time when the Jews of the East
End were popularly identified with "sweated labor" (both as
workers and as employers), and when there were vociferous
demands to limit or prohibit their immigration and even to
expel them, the essay was almost philosemitic. It is a remarkable
document, remarkable not only for its account of the practices
and beliefs, the manners and morals, of this generation of immigrant Jews, but also for its revelation of the attitudes and values
of at least one shrewd and unsentimental English observer.

The essay opens with a brief historical account of the several waves of Jewish immigrants who came to England in modern times, most recently from Poland and Russia. It describes
the institutions devised by them to provide for their religious
and communal needs: the Board of Deputies, recognized by
the government as the official representative body; the Beth
Din, which administered religious law; the Board of Guardians,
which coordinated relief and social services; and the synagogues,
catering to the various classes of Jews, of varying religious
practices and commitments. It is a notably sympathetic account
of the difficult circumstances under which the Jews came to
England and of the community they created in that alien land.

If there are expressions in this account that a sensitive
reader might interpret as snide or disparaging, it is because the
reader is unfamiliar with Beatrice Webb's own values and rhetoric. When she commends, for example, the Jewish Board of
Deputies for "the skill, the tenacity, and above all, the admirable
temper with which our Hebrew fellow-countrymen have insinuated themselves into the life of the nation, without forsaking
the faith of their forefathers or sacrificing as a community the
purity of their race," there is nothing suspect in the term
"purity of their race." To Mrs. Webb, as to most Victorians,

"race" was an innocent word and "purity of race" an admirable ideal. Nor was the word "insinuated" meant to be pejorative; the Fabians commonly used it to describe their own political strategy. "I could insinuate myself," Beatrice Webb once boasted, "into smoking-rooms, business offices, private and public conferences, without rousing suspicion."

After a moving description of the Polish Jew who "suffers oppression and bears ridicule with imperturbable good humor" and remains silent in "the face of insult and abuse," she put the rhetorical questions: "For why resent when your object is to overcome? Why bluster and fight when you may manipulate or control in secret?" These last sentences have been cited as "clearly anti-Semitic," in suggesting something like a Jewish conspiracy against Western society. But this was not at all Mrs. Webb's intention. In fact she was praising, not disparaging the Jew. For this too was the conscious policy of the Fabians: to "overcome" by quiet persistence, to "manipulate or control in secret"

Beatrice Webb herself had a strong religious streak, so it is not surprising to find her appreciative of Judaism, all the more because she saw Judaism as her kind of religion, a preeminently this-worldly religion. The strength of the Jewish religion, she said, was that it provided "a law of life on this earth, sanctioned by the rewards and punishments of this world." The Beth Din, for example, adjudicated not only questions of *kashruth* but also family quarrels, trade and labor disputes, breach-of-promise suits, and the myriad issues that arose in everyday life.

Thus too the local community organization, or *chevrah*

(she used that word to describe both the group and its meeting place), was part synagogue, part school, part social center, part benefit club assisting its members in times of sickness or death. She described the efforts of some well-intentioned leaders of the Anglo-Jewish establishment to replace the small, overcrowded, unsanitary *chevrahs* by a single grand synagogue, and was pleased to report that wiser counsels prevailed and the idea was abandoned. Sanitation and crowding were relative matters, she observed, and in this case the smallness and closeness of the *chevrahs* were more virtues than vices. For they were "self-creating, self-supporting, and self-governing communities; small enough to generate public opinion and the practical supervision of private morals, and large enough to stimulate charity, worship, and study by communion and example."

There was a still poorer class of Jews, she pointed out, who did not belong to any *chevrah* but who nevertheless clung "with an almost superstitious tenacity to the habits and customs of their race." Although the class itself was permanent, the individuals composing it were in a constant state of flux, the older immigrants rising out of it while newer immigrants were entering it. But even this lowest class was not without resources, for it was "united to the Jewish middle and upper class by a downward stream of charity and personal service, a benevolence at once so widespread and so thoroughgoing, that it fully justifies the saying, 'All Israel are brethren.'"

Jewish benevolence was also of a special kind. The Jewish "Free School," she said, was the largest school of its kind in all of England, "a striking example of the admirable organization peculiar to Jewish charity." And the Jewish Board of Guardians was unlike any of the other Boards of Guardians that supervised the distribution of public relief. Privately organized and financed, it raised £13,000 to £14,000 annually, of which only £2,000 was given in the familiar form of poor relief – money or vouchers for the purchase of coal, clothes, or other necessities. Smaller sums went for emigration, sanitary inspection, special workrooms for girls, and the like. Well over half was given to individuals for trade and business, most of it in the form of capital. The intention was to enable the recipients to become self-supporting, and the success of this policy was such that of the 3,313 cases handled by the board in 1887, only 268 had previously been applicants. Thus there was not in the Jewish community, Mrs. Webb observed, as there was in England at large, a "chronically parasitic class of 'paupers.'" Either because of "the character of those who take" or "the method of those who give," Jewish charity did not have the demoralizing effects that relief had on the rest of the population.

"Every country," Beatrice Webb cited the familiar saying, "has the Jew it deserves." In the case of England, she maintained, this was patently untrue, for England received its most recent contingent of Jews "readymade" from a country diametrically different from itself. Because one could not understand the peculiarities of English Jews without knowing something of the country they came from, Mrs. Webb interrupted her account of the English Jewish community to describe the conditions in Russia, where "oppression and restriction have assumed every conceivable form." There no Jew could own land or, often, rent it; in one place he could not enter a profession, in another he could not establish a business, in still others he had no right of domicile; and everywhere he was subject to religious and social persecution, living "in daily terror of the petty tyranny of a capricious governor." Yet in spite of this "systematic oppression," the Jews multiplied and prospered in every trade and profession open to them. Even the penal laws were ineffectual against the "superior mental equipment" of the Jews, driving them into "low channels of parasitic activity," where they survived sometimes to the detriment of their "Christian fellow-subjects." Finally, the Russian government changed its tactics and deliberately encouraged "mob violence of a brutal and revolting character" as a means of expulsion.

It was this history of oppression and persecution, described with brutal candor but also compassion, that Beatrice Webb saw as the formative experience of the latest generation of Jewish immigrants. Their adversities were the source of their virtues. "Social isolation has perfected home life; persecution has intensified religious fervor; an existence of unremitting toil, and rigid observance of the moral precepts and sanitary and dietary regulations of the Jewish religion have favored the growth of sobriety, personal purity, and a consequent power of physical endurance." Having lived among a half-civilized people and been deprived of a secular education, they focused all their thoughts and feelings in the literature of their race, "in the Old Testament, with its magnificent promises of universal dominion; in the Talmud, with its minute instructions as to the means of gaining it." The child on its mother's lap lisped passages from the Talmud; the old man tottering to his grave still sought in it the secret of existence. The Talmud, Mrs. Webb quoted a Jewish authority of the time, was "an encyclopedia of law, civil and penal, ecclesiastical and international, human and divine" – in effect, a Jewish *Corpus Juris*. Beyond that law, "the pious Israelite recognizes no obligations; the laws and customs of the Christians are so many regulations to be obeyed, evaded, set at naught, or used according to the possibilities and expediencies of the hour."

It is curious to find this mixture of idealized romanticism – the child on its mother's lap (surely it should be its father's) lisping portions of the Talmud – and plainspoken realism – Christian laws to be obeyed or evaded as expediency dictated. To Mrs. Webb they were opposite sides of the same coin: the same circumstances that made the Jews so meticulous in the observance of their own laws, customs, and obligations made them less than respectful of the laws, customs, and obligations of Christian societies, where they had managed to survive a long history of persecution only by a strategy of obedience, evasion, or violation. She hastened to add that she was speaking only of the recent immigrants who were fresh from those foreign experiences, not of the older Jewish community which had long enjoyed "the freedom, the culture, and the public spirit of English life."

The process of acculturation, as she described it, was rapid. The "greenest" of the immigrants eked out a bare existence either from the charity of coreligionists or by working day and night for a small contractor in return for a place to sleep and a loaf of bread. After a few weeks or months, having learned a trade, the worker found a job where he received some pittance of pay. Within a year he joined a *chevrah*, and, if he managed to resist the "Jewish passion for gambling," he was on his way to becoming a petty trader or a "tiny capitalist," earning a living by his own labor and that of a few employees. He then found lodging in a "model dwelling" (a privately financed housing project) where he and his family lived comfortably and decently. At this point Mrs. Webb's picture verges on the idyllic. "He treats his wife with courtesy and tenderness, and they discuss constantly the future of the children." He never goes to a public house, although he does sometimes enjoy a glass of rum and a game of cards with friends. "In short, he has become a law-abiding and self-respecting citizen of our great metropolis, and feels himself the equal of a Montefiore or a Rothschild."

This achievement was all the greater, according to Mrs. Webb, because it was in stark contrast to the "drunkenness, immorality, and gambling" that infected the East End. Set in the midst of the "very refuse of our civilization," the Jewish workers moved upward and onward, leaving to others the poorest jobs, the worst workshops, the dirtiest lodgings. Why was it, Mrs. Webb asked, that they were so successful? And why was that success so resented by the Christians with whom they came into contact?

One of the things that distinguished the Jewish immigrant from the English laborer, Mrs. Webb insisted, was his intellect. "The poorest Jew has inherited through the medium of his religion a trained intellect." Unlike Christian nations with their sharp class distinctions, "the children of Israel are a nation of priests." From earliest childhood a Jew was taught the rites and ceremonies, the laws and poetry of his people; he learned to master an ancient tongue and comprehend the subtleties and "fantasies" of the Talmud. He was not, to be sure, "cultured" in the sense of having a wide knowledge and appreciation of the cultural experiences of others; on the contrary, his focus was entirely on the past and present of his own race. But his intellectual faculties – memory, reason, calculation – were highly cultivated.

This was true among all classes of Jews, with the result that there was a striking equality among them, a uniformly high, if narrow, level of intellectual training. And these intellectual accomplishments, originating in their religious training, were intensified by a process of natural selection, the long history of

persecution having the effect of weeding out the less competent and the less intelligent. Thus the Jewish workers in the
East End were "a race of brain-workers," in contrast to the non-
Jews, who constituted "a class of manual labourers." For Jews,
manual labor was "the first rung of the social ladder, to be
superseded or supplanted on the first opportunity by the esti-
mates of the profit-maker, the transactions of the dealer, or the
calculations of the money-lender" – provided, of course, that
they did not fall prey to that "vice of the intellect," gambling.

Their intellectual superiority, Mrs. Webb explained, was
only one factor contributing to their success. More important
was the "moral and physical regimen" that every pious Jew,
male and female, was subjected to from birth – a regimen that
"favors the full development of the bodily organs, protects them
from abuse and disease, and stimulates the growth of physical
self-control and mental endurance." Unlike Christianity or
Buddhism, which seek spiritual exaltation through the mortifi-
cation of the flesh, the religious and dietary laws of Judaism
"accentuate the physical aspect of life"; they are intended not
as a preparation for another world but as a "course of training
adapted to prolong the life of the individual and to multiply
the number of his descendants." This moral discipline was
naturally centered on the family; it prescribed obedience toward
parents, devotion to children, chastity for the girl, and support
and protection for the wife. Thus the religious Jew was "a
being at once moral and sensual; a creature endowed with the
power of physical endurance, but gifted with a highly-trained
and well-regulated appetite for sensuous enjoyment."

It was this combination of intellectual aptitude, moral recti-
tude, and physical stamina that accounted for the Jew's success.
And it was the fact of his success that exposed him to oppression and ridicule, insult and injury, all of which he endured

with "imperturbable good humor." Unfettered by any fixed standard of living, he adjusted readily to opportunity; he was neither "depressed by penury" nor "demoralized by gain." Unmoved by the passions that led to drink or crime, by the humors that came from "unsatisfied emotions," he could pursue his purposes without distraction or despair. Thus, Mrs. Webb concluded:

> *Is it surprising that in this 19th century, with its ideal of physical health, intellectual acquisition, and material prosperity, the chosen people, with three thousand years of training, should in some instances realize the promise made by Moses to their forefathers: "Thou shalt drive out nations mightier than thyself, and thou shalt take their land as an inheritance?"*

That rhetorical question would seem to be sufficient answer both to Beatrice Webb's first question – Why was the immigrant Jew so successful? – and to her second – Why was that success so resented by others? But she went on to propose another reason for that resentment. The immigrant Jew, it appeared, for all his virtues, was deficient in "that highest and latest development of human sentiment – social morality." She hastily explained that she did not mean that the Jews violated the laws and conventions of either social or commercial life. On the contrary, they were among the most law-abiding inhabitants of the East End. "They keep the peace, they pay their debts, and they abide by their contracts; practices in which they are undoubtedly superior to the English and Irish casual laborers among whom they dwell." They did so for good reason, because they knew that " 'law and order' and the 'sanctity of contract' are the sine qua non of a full and free competition in the open market," and that they themselves could succeed "by competition, and by competition alone." Her father, she wrote in her autobiography, "believed in the Jewish maxim – a maxim he often cited – that a bargain is not a good bargain unless it pays both sides."

But while the foreign Jew, in contrast to the native-born, acculturated Jew, observed the law and the sanctity of contract, he was unrestrained by considerations of personal dignity, class loyalty, or trade integrity. The small manufacturer often rose to the rank of capitalist by bad and dishonest production; the petty dealer or money-lender, intent upon buying cheap and selling dear, took advantage of the weaknesses of his customers; the worker, trying to become a small master, was prepared to underbid his fellow workers. "In short, the foreign Jew totally ignores all social obligations other than keeping the law of the land, the maintenance of his own family, and the charitable relief of co-religionists."

It was a subtle point Mrs. Webb was making, for within the same paragraph she described the immigrants as scrupulous in obeying the law and abiding by contracts, knowing these to be the conditions of a free, open, and competitive economy, and thus of their own success. Yet a few sentences later she charged them with producing inferior goods, taking advantage of their customers, and ignoring "all social obligations." These social, as distinct from legal, obligations were obviously meant to signify a more sophisticated, civilized order of obligation, one that came more naturally to Englishmen than to foreigners, especially foreigners whose survival had not allowed them the luxury of such niceties.

It was this distinction that Maurice Samuel was to describe so poignantly in *The Gentleman and the Jew* (1950), which drew upon his own experiences as an immigrant trying to accommodate to English society. (Samuel came to England as a child from Romania a dozen years after Beatrice Webb wrote her essay.) No one has ever mistaken an Eastern European immigrant Jew for an English gentleman. What is interesting about Mrs. Webb's account is not so much the failure of the Jew to reach that highest level of "social morality" characteristic of the gentlemanly ethos, as his success in reaching the not inconsiderable level of personal and communal morality that she associated with the Jewish ethos.

What is also interesting is her identification of that Jewish ethos with the ethos of capitalism. The final paragraph of her essay makes the point explicitly and sympathetically:

> *Thus the immigrant Jew, fresh from the sorrowful experiences typical of the history of his race, seems to justify by his existence those strange assumptions which figured for man in the political economy of [David] Ricardo – an Always Enlightened Selfishness [these last words capitalized], seeking employment or profit with an absolute mobility of body and mind, without pride, without preference, without interests outside the struggle for the existence and welfare of the individual and the family.*

The Jew as "economic man." Where have we heard that before? From Marx, for one, whose essay "On the Jewish Question," published in 1844, has had more echoes in the socialist movement than some socialists would like to think. There has been much controversy about whether that essay is antisemitic or simply anticapitalist; but since Marx equates the Jew with the capitalist – not accidentally or circumstantially but metaphysically and religiously – the distinction is academic. "Money is the jealous god of Israel before whom no other god may exist.... The god of the Jews has been secularized and has become the god of the world. The bill of exchange is the Jew's actual god."

It is interesting to compare Marx and Beatrice Webb on this subject. Both portray the Jew as economic man, but how different the image is in the two cases. Mrs. Webb was, if not a full-fledged socialist, then at least an incipient socialist. But she was a *Victorian* socialist, and at this time a Victorian more than a socialist. It was the Victorian in her that responded favorably to those values – hard work, thrift, intelligence, sobriety, fidelity, self-reliance, self-discipline, devotion to family, loyalty to community, respect for law – which she saw as conducive to economic and social improvement and to a decent, moral existence. Her economic man, the economic man she identified with the Jew, exemplified an "always enlightened selfishness" – enlightened because his "selfishness" embraced his family and community. He took upon himself, for example, the care of the poorer members of his community, promoting values that were not only in his self-interest but also good in themselves.

There was, by contrast, nothing "enlightened" about Marx's economic man. The key word Marx used to describe him was "alienated." The Jew was dominated by an "alien essence"; his religion was a fraud and an illusion; his only god was money and the bill of exchange. As for his much-vaunted family life – the wife, for example, whom Mrs. Webb depicted as loved, protected, and respected – according to Marx that wife was nothing more than an "object of commerce," a woman to be "bought and sold."

If Beatrice Webb's portrait of the Jew-*qua*-economic man is so different from Marx's, it is not only because she was a Victorian, thus almost by definition a moralist, but also because she was deeply religious. One of the great tragedies of her life was that she was never able to reconcile religion and socialism – the religion that she believed to be the metaphysical and emotional mainstay of life, the end and purpose of existence; and the socialism that she saw as the science of social engineering, the rational means of reforming and reorganizing society for the greatest good of all. But whatever her failure to reconcile the two, her own sense of religiosity was deep and enduring. She regularly prayed at home and less regularly, but often enough, attended services and took communion at St. Paul's. Thus she could respect, even admire, the Jew who also prayed, attended services, and observed the laws and rites of his religion. Religion was no "illusion" to her, not her own religion or anyone else's.

She also appreciated, as even a great many nonbelieving Victorians did, the relationship between religion and morality. Valuing morality as highly as the Victorians did – valuing it even, as I have said, when they violated it – they welcomed any support for morality. And traditionally the strongest support, the ultimate sanction, came from religion. For Mrs. Webb, Judaism was an especially effective instrument of morality because it was a this-worldly religion. In this sense, Judaism transcended the duality that she found so disturbing in her own life, the duality between religion and socialism, between ultimate ends and proximate means. In Judaism, as she saw it, there was no such dichotomy. Life was all of a piece – ritual and law, individual and community, personal salvation and social obligation, moral conduct and economic advancement.

This is Beatrice Webb describing the Jewish immigrant community in England in the late nineteenth century. I do not know how credible her account is. I have no reason *not* to credit it, although I am suspicious of some of her more effusive statements and sweeping generalizations. There were surely Jews who were drunkards as well as gamblers (the only vice she allowed them), who abandoned their wives and children, who did not support their poorer brethren, who never rose above the lower rungs of the economic ladder, who were not notably intelligent, or moral, or successful. There were also, as she must have known, Jews for whom success was an invitation to cease being Jews. But these, by all accounts, constituted a relatively small number of the Jewish immigrants, and a still smaller number relative to the non-Jewish laborers of the East End. And even these Jewish deviants, so to speak, did not challenge the ethos; they only violated it, from weakness of character or misfortunes of circumstance.

But whether and to what extent the Jews actually conformed to the ethos Mrs. Webb attributed to them, there is little doubt of the nature of that ethos or of her own esteem for it. Nor is there any doubt that this is remarkably akin to the ethos Margaret Thatcher has in mind when she calls for a return to "Victorian values." Mrs. Thatcher would not like to be compared with Mrs. Webb, and for good reason. I myself find it odd to be writing of Mrs. Webb as warmly as I am now doing. But whatever other reservations I may have about her, I do appreciate (as the Anglo-Jewish press did at the time) her sympathetic portrait of Jewish immigrants in an alien country, stoically, courageously coping with poverty and adversity. And I appreciate even more her sympathetic account of the ethic that governed their behavior and the religion that inspired that ethic.

That ethic is more familiar to us today under the label of the Protestant or Puritan ethic. When Max Weber popularized these terms in 1904, in the first of his essays later published under the title *The Protestant Ethic and the Spirit of Capitalism*, he mentioned Judaism only in passing, and only to distinguish between the Judaic ethic, which encouraged a "speculatively oriented adventurous capitalism," and the Puritan ethic, which was the source of the more rational "bourgeois capitalistic ethic." Seven years later Werner Sombart described essentially the same ethic, attributing it to the Jews, in his provocative book *The Jews and Modern Capitalism*. By now the subject has become one of the staples of historical controversy. The terms of the debate shift and blur, Protestantism mutating into Calvinism, Calvinism into Puritanism, Puritanism into Judaism, Judaism into the Judaic-Christian tradition. And the relation between the terms changes. Sometimes it is the religious ethos that is thought to inspire capitalism; sometimes capitalism that is presumed to determine the religious ethos; sometimes a secular ethos that is said to shape both religion and capitalism.

I do not propose to enter into any of these controversies. Certainly I would not say, as Sombart did, that "Puritanism *is* Judaism," or, as Weber is sometimes accused of saying, that the Protestant ethic *caused* the rise of capitalism. Nor would I venture any opinion on whether the Judaic ethic derived primarily from Mosaic and Talmudic law or from the historical experience of the Jews. For my purposes here, what is interesting about the ethos of this Jewish community in the 1880s is its relation to the Victorian ethos, and this, in turn, to the capitalist ethos.

It is ironic that this study of the Jews should have been written by a woman who was even then sympathetic to socialism and who, after she became a committed socialist, continued to cherish the values – capitalist values, as she herself recognized –

that she had found among those poor Jewish immigrants. It is as if she wanted to superimpose those values upon socialism itself; as if the values that make for a successful, and ethical, capitalism are also required for a successful, and ethical, socialism. The very idea, of course, is self-contradictory. An ethic of "always enlightened selfishness" predicates, as Ricardo said, "an absolute mobility of body and mind." It is a free, competitive, acquisitive ethic, placing no limits, apart from those set by law and religion, upon the exertions or sacrifices an individual chooses to make or the commensurate rewards he expects to receive. It encourages workers to earn as much as they are capable of earning, to save as much of their earnings as they think proper, to invest their savings in enterprises they hope will be profitable, to reap the profits of those enterprises and pass them on to their families, and to discharge their communal responsibilities in accord with their religious precepts and voluntary desires. Such an ethic is hardly compatible with the kind of planned, controlled, regulated – regimented, an unfriendly critic might call it – society that was the avowed aim of Fabian socialism, to say nothing of Marxism.

Mrs. Thatcher has no such problem. Her Victorian values are entirely compatible with capitalism as she envisages it – and with the Jewish ethos as Beatrice Webb described it. When Mrs. Thatcher wants to epitomize those values, she cites the famous sermon by John Wesley on "The Use of Money," delivered, incidentally, before his almost entirely working-class flock. "Gain all you can," he exhorted them. "Save all you can. Give all you can." That is pretty close to the ethic Beatrice Webb ascribed to the Jews – including the last part of that trinity, "Give all you can."

It may be said that this is not an exalted or heroic ethic. That is certainly true. But those of us who have had some experience of exalted and heroic ethics may be reassured by the modesty of this one. A philosophy of "always enlightened selfishness" does not sound as inspiring as a philosophy of "always altruistic socialism," but it turns out to be a good deal more humane in practice. One is no longer surprised at the failure of socialistic experiments; one would not be terribly distressed if they merely failed. What *is* distressing is the fact that all too often they succeed all too well – succeed in establishing and perpetuating a regime that is anything but altruistic, that is, in fact, oppressive and tyrannical.

A regime based upon the ethic of "always enlightened selfishness" has the undeniable advantages of producing a more efficient and prosperous economy and a freer polity and society. It is also, I would venture to say, more genuinely, as distinct from rhetorically, moral, because it requires no violation or transformation of human nature. It takes people as they are and as they always have been, capable of being enlightened as well as selfish – enlightened precisely because they are selfish, because their "self" naturally embraces family and community, religion and tradition, interests and values.

If this is a capitalist ethos, it is also a democratic ethos. Those modest, mundane, lowly virtues – hard work, sobriety, frugality, foresight – are within the capacity of everyone. They do not assume any special breeding, or social status, or talent, or valor, or grace, or even money. They are common virtues within the reach of common people. They are preeminently democratic virtues.

They are also (in the old sense of the term) *liberal* virtues. By putting a premium on ordinary virtues attainable by ordinary people, the ethos locates responsibility and authority within each individual. In an aristocratic age, only the exceptional, heroic individual was seen as a free moral agent, the master of his fate. Now all individuals are assumed to be free moral agents, hence their own masters. It is no accident that the Victorian ethos put such a premium on the self: self-interest, self-help, self-control, self-reliance, self-respect, self-discipline. A liberal society, the Victorians believed, requires a moral citizenry. The more effective the voluntary exercise of morality on the part of each individual and the more internalized that morality, the less need there is for the external, coercive instruments of the state. Just as law, in a civilized society, is a substitute for coercion, so morality is a surrogate for authority.

Yesterday's liberalism is today's conservatism. Today it is Mrs. Thatcher, the leader of the Conservative Party, who has reaffirmed those Victorian values in the name (as she told the Church of Scotland elders) of the "Judaic-Christian tradition." Recalling Mrs. Webb's account of the Jewish community, we may be forgiven for thinking that she regarded those Victorian values as perhaps more Judaic than Christian.

1989

CHAPTER NINETEEN

For the Love of Country: Civil Society and the State

———————■|||||■———————

THE ERA OF big government is over," President Clinton announced in his State of the Union address in January 1995, responding to the mandate of the people as expressed in the newly elected Republican Congress. That statement has proved to be so false – look only at Clinton's proposals for educational reforms, which would enhance rather than diminish the role of government – that one may overlook how misleading it is in another respect. For "big government" is a euphemism for the current, much-expanded version of the "welfare state." And it was this that the American people had rejected.

Big government is objectionable not only because it is big but because it is bad. The English, who have had more experience with it than we have, call it the "nanny state." It treats individuals not as adults but as wayward and improvident children who require the constant supervision and protection of their guardians – which is to say, legislators, bureaucrats, social workers. Such a state is inefficient, costly, cumbersome, corrupt, but these are the least of its vices. Its real offense is that it is demeaning and demoralizing to those who come under its not-too-tender embrace.

To reduce the role of the state, conservatives, and many liberals as well, are now seeking to restore and revitalize the institutions of civil society – family, community, church, local associations, private enterprises – in the hope that there, in the intimate, personal relations of daily life, individuals will be able to function as free, responsible, moral adults. This is an admirable idea, and one that deserves to be put at the top of the political agenda. It will take, to be sure, a good deal of ingenuity and determination to carry it out. We will have to go beyond the current strategy of the "devolution" of welfare to the states and devolve it further to civil society, thus making "welfare" the ultimate responsibility of families, communities, and charities.

We will also have to divest ourselves of unrealistic expectations about civil society itself. Some families are too dysfunctional to perform the roles assigned to them, or, if not actually dysfunctional, then so weakened by divorce, serial cohabitation, and single parenthood as to be of little avail in the task ahead. So too, private and communal associations, even many churches, are so permeated by the dominant cultural values that they can hardly serve as paragons of morality and responsibility. It is evidently not enough to revitalize civil society; we have the far more difficult task of remoralizing it.

But there is an additional problem. The enlarged welfare state has not only denigrated individuals; it has denigrated the state itself by reducing it to the role of *in loco parentis* and obliging it to assume the domestic, "nurturing" tasks of parents and families. In effect, it has depoliticized the state, depriving it of its unique and essential political nature. By the same token, it has depoliticized the citizenry, depriving the people of their proper role in a political community – indeed, of their very identity as citizens.

The proponents of civil society, in their eagerness to do away with the nanny state, may run the same risk – of belittling, even delegitimizing, the state itself, and in the process subverting the idea of citizenship. In the new dispensation, the inhabitants of civil society, released from the bondage of the welfare state, will no longer be subjects or dependents. But neither will they be citizens in the classic, political sense of that word. They will simply be inhabitants of civil society, as individuals, family members, neighbors, parishioners, workers or employers, constituents of one or another "voluntary association," as Tocqueville put it. As such, they will care for themselves and for one another, for the young, the old, and the infirm, providing for their needs and amenities. Unlike the infantilized subjects of the nanny state, they will be adults, with the rights and obligations, the satisfactions and duties, of responsible, moral individuals.

That is all to the good, and infinitely better than our present situation. But it is not enough. For there is another dimension of adulthood lacking here, and that is the political. Aristotle reminds us that man is "born for citizenship"; he is "by nature a political animal." Not a "social animal," as this phrase is often mistranslated. It is not in the "household" or in the "village," Aristotle says, but only in the *polis* that man is truly human, decisively different from "bees or any other gregarious animals." Bees and animals, after all, also inhabit households and villages. They provide shelter and sustenance for themselves and their young; they even have social relations and social structures. They have something like civil society. What they do not have is a polity, a government of laws and institutions by means of which – and only by means of which, Aristotle believed – man consciously, rationally tries to establish a just regime and pursue the good life.

———

I may be especially sensitive to the apolitical, even in some instances antipolitical, aspect of civil society because I have encountered it before, in quite another context. Decades ago, before politicians and political scientists discovered the virtues of civil society, historians discovered the virtues of social history – "history," as it has been called, "with the politics left out." This was history "from below," not the "elitist" history that focuses on great events, great ideas, and great men (or even great women), but the history of ordinary people in their ordinary lives. The subjects of the new history – the poor, women, minorities, blacks – had been omitted or "marginalized" in the old history, it was said, because they played no conspicuous role in politics. To bring them onto center stage and give them starring roles, history itself had to be depoliticized. Thus, where the old history took place primarily in the political arena, the new history focuses on the home, family, community, workplace – in short, on civil society.

The effect of the new history has been not only to depoliticize history but to deaggrandize it as well, to shift attention from great, public, historic events and personages to the daily lives of the "anonymous masses." The new historians pride themselves on "deprivileging" the great and restoring the existential reality of life for ordinary people. An American historian has explained why politics is of little importance: "Have not the vast majority of people in the past thought that where they lived and how they made a living, who they married, and what happened to their children rather more 'basic and significant' than who won the last election?'"

But is it not a new and more demeaning kind of condescension to assume that the vast majority of people are less interested in "who won the last election" than, say, a Harvard professor, who can somehow manage to be interested in national politics without neglecting his home, career, or family? And is not politics itself – not only "the last election" but the democratic system that sustains and validates elections – of vital importance to the lives of all Americans, and perhaps to "ordinary" people more than to the "elite" because their freedom, rights, even their livelihood are more intimately bound up with the democratic political process?

Some of the enthusiasts for civil society may be falling into the trap of the social historians, of unwittingly disparaging those they respect and giving credibility to those they distrust. One of the unfortunate consequences of the welfare state is that it has exacerbated the anarchic impulse in American society. The bureaucratic bullies of the left give a semblance of plausibility to terrorists of the right. Today more than ever, when there are so many legitimate grievances against government, we cannot afford to delegitimize legitimate government.

Nor can we afford the luxury of being apolitical, of depriving ourselves of the proper resources of government. Indeed, civil society itself requires them, if only to preserve its independence, strengthen its constituent parts, and thus help remoralize itself. A sensible tax policy could encourage two-parent families, as it currently encourages home ownership. Divorce laws could be devised to deter the breakup of the family, rather than, as at present, facilitating it. The courts could support the rights of communities to enforce ordinances against pornography, obscenity, or abortion (as they did for much of our history). And if the courts are recalcitrant, the legislature could act more vigorously to achieve these ends.

What is required, in short, is a delicate balancing act: to discredit and dismantle the welfare state while retaining a healthy respect for the state itself and its institutions. In much the same way, critics of the Clinton administration have the task of exposing the legal and moral corruption of the president and his associates, without detracting from the dignity and legitimacy of the presidency itself – indeed, pursuing the former all the more vigorously in order to preserve the latter.

But something even more important is at stake in the denigration of the state. "Citizenship," in discussions of civil society, is all too often reduced to civility and sociability. Good citizens are good neighbors: they attend PTA meetings, donate blood, curb their dogs, are courteous and considerate. These are no mean virtues; in our time, they are very considerable virtues. But they are not the only virtues associated with citizenship. Some virtues – ambition, zeal, energy, venturesomeness, leadership, and heroism – transcend family and community. These are outsized virtues that may only be realized on a national or even international scale. The qualities that make for good neighbors do not necessarily make for great leaders, still less for heroes.

The devaluing of these virtues impoverishes not only society as a whole but also those individuals who do not themselves aspire to them, who make no claim to eminence. Hegel, who is better known for his praise of "world-historical individuals," nevertheless appreciated the need of ordinary citizens for a spirit that elevates them above their ordinary lives. Civil society, he said (long before Tocqueville popularized the idea), is that "territory of mediation" where people, in addition to satisfying their needs, begin to overcome their "particularity" by experiencing themselves as more than isolated individuals. But only in the state, he insisted, do they truly fulfill themselves and transcend their particularity by being identified with something larger than themselves, with the "Spirit" or "Idea" manifest in the state.

Americans have never been comfortable with terms like "Spirit" or "Idea," especially as applied to the state. But we do understand and respect the ideas of nationality and patriotism. "Statecraft," as George Will said, is a form of "soulcraft"; it helps shape the character, and hence the soul, of a people. Of a people, not merely of individuals. And not merely the character of a people but its very identity, its sense of nationality and its spirit of patriotism. This, finally, is what we are in danger of losing – and again, today more than ever.

Paradoxically, the collapse of Communism, far from invigorating us as a nation triumphant over an "evil empire," seems to have left us demoralized and purposeless. The absence of any external threat to the country, a welfare state woefully deficient in soulcraft, a multiculturalism that has fragmented society, and a postmodernism that has deconstructed the culture – the combination is proving nearly fatal to our sense of national identity and pride.

Civil society is the least of the culprits in this regard, but it can unwittingly contribute to the same effect. It is natural and commendable for individuals to seek satisfaction in their families and communities, to make these the center of their emotional ties and moral commitments. But to feel completely fulfilled in these roles and entirely identified with them is to lose that larger sense of national identity which comes not from civil society but from the state and the polity. Today, when politics has been so tainted by cynicism and scandal, and when the state itself has been so perverted by the politics of welfare, the retreat to private and communal life is all too understandable. But it would be most unfortunate if it were to deprive the state of the services, the resources, and the loyalties of its citizens, in peacetime and, more urgently, in wartime.

Why compete for national office and take up residence in Washington, if all one's values and interests are centered on one's family and community? Why support a strong national defense and a vigorous foreign policy designed to maintain America's supremacy, if one's commitments are entirely local? Why, in times of national emergency, take up arms and possibly give one's life, if one has so tenuous a relationship to the country as a whole – if there is so little sense of a national interest requiring that ultimate sacrifice?

———

The phrase "little platoon," coined two centuries ago by Edmund Burke, has become one of the watchwords of civil society. But the context in which that phrase appears is rarely quoted:

> *To be attached to the subdivision, to love the little platoon we belong to in society, is the first principle (the germ as it were) of public affections. It is the first link in the series by which we proceed towards a love to our country, and to mankind.*

And again:

> *We begin our public affections in our families. . . . We pass on to our neighborhoods and our habitual provincial connections. . . . Perhaps it is a sort of elemental training*

to those higher and more large regards, by which alone men come to be affected, as with their own concern, in the prosperity of a kingdom.

Civil society, Burke teaches us, is a two-way street. It takes us back to our roots, to our nearest and dearest. But it should also take us forward to our nation and country. Love of country – the expression now sounds almost archaic – is an ennobling sentiment, quite as ennobling as love of family and community. It elevates us, invests our daily life with a larger meaning, dignifies the individual even as it humanizes politics. Civil society should not be the enemy of the state but its ally – an ally not of the welfare state, to be sure, but of a state worthy of our "public affections."

1997

CHAPTER TWENTY

From Postmodernism
to Transgenderism

—————■■■■■■————

THE Caitlyn (née Bruce) Jenner case has engendered, if not a new subject, at least a newly publicized and sensationalized one. For an old-timer like myself, transgenderism recalls the postmodernism that swept the universities several decades ago, suggesting a new postmodernism – a post-postmodernism – more dramatic, audacious, and perhaps perilous than the old. It might be instructive to look back to the old, if only as a cautionary tale, mindful of its aspirations but also its tribulations.

In an article written almost twenty years ago, I tried to put postmodernism in historical perspective. That perspective is even more germane to transgenderism today.

Imported from France (which had acquired it from Germany), postmodernism made its appearance in the United States in the 1970s, first in departments of literature and then in other disciplines of the humanities. Its forefathers are Nietzsche and Heidegger, its fathers Derrida and Foucault. From Jacques Derrida postmodernism has borrowed the vocabulary of deconstruction: the "aporia" (the dubious or enigmatic nature) of discourse, the "indeterminacy" of language, the "fictive" nature of signs and symbols, the self-referential character of words and their dissociation from any presumed reality, the "problematization" of all subjects, events, and texts. From Michel Foucault it has adopted the focus on power: words and ideas as a means of "privileging" the "hegemonic" groups in society, and knowledge itself an instrument and product of the "power structure." Thus traditional discourse and learning are impugned as "logocentric" (dominated by the word), "phallocentric" (dominated by the male), and "totalizing" or "authoritarian" (in the presumption that reality can be contained and comprehended).

In literature, postmodernism entails the denial of the fixity of any text (not only the immutability of meaning but the immutability of the text itself); of the authority of the author over the critic or reader in determining the substance and meaning of the text; of any canon of great books and, more significantly, of the very idea of greatness. In philosophy, it is a denial of the constancy of language, of any correspondence between language and reality, of any proximate truth about reality, indeed, of any essential reality. In history, it is a denial of the objectivity of the historian, of the factuality or reality of the past, and thus of the possibility of arriving at any truths about the past. For all disciplines it induces a radical skepticism, relativism, and subjectivism that denies not this or that truth about any subject but the very idea of truth – that denies even the ideal of truth, truth as something to aspire to even if it can never be fully attained.

228

Derrida's *Of Grammatology*, which in 1967 introduced the concept of deconstructionism, is now regarded as one of the founding documents of postmodernism. The preface by the translator is euphoric: "The fall into the abyss of deconstruction inspires us with as much pleasure as fear. We are intoxicated with the prospect of never hitting bottom." Almost half a century later, the striking image of the abyss was evoked for another postmodernist eminence, Paul de Man, Derrida's friend and colleague at Yale. De Man, his biographer tells us, was "the only man who ever looked into the abyss and came away smiling."

The abyss that de Man confronted, and came away from smiling, was the Holocaust. After his death in 1983, it was revealed that during the war de Man had written hundreds of antisemitic articles for a pro-Nazi journal in Belgium (and had led a rather unsavory life in general, including criminal financial dealings and a bigamous marriage). Even more revealing than his antisemitism was the response of other postmodernists. The "soft deconstructionists" (as they called themselves) dissociated themselves from de Man, although not from postmodernism. But the "hard" ones, including Derrida, hotly defended him, not on the grounds that the antisemitic articles were an unfortunate youthful lapse (he was then well into his twenties), but by deconstructing those "texts" until they appeared to say very nearly the opposite of what they obviously said.

The de Man affair was a wake-up call for postmodernism – and for its present manifestation in transgenderism. As postmodernism had made its way through the university deconstructing one after another of the humanities, so it now seems to be deconstructing humanity itself. The "indeterminacy" and "problematization" of the disciplines, the denial of the "fixity" and "immutability" of "texts," indeed, the denial of any "essential reality" in the postmodernist "project" (as we now say) may be reflected in a similar denial of reality in the transgenderist project.

The transgenderist would protest that it was not a denial but precisely an affirmation of reality that was being sought, a sexual reality that had been obscured or belied by the accident of birth. To which a skeptic might reply that reality, once deconstructed, is not so easily reconstructed. The fact that transgenderism requires for its completion not only hormonal treatment but nothing less than genital surgery may induce serious second thoughts. The removal – the deconstruction, so to speak – of the very organs that define gender and enable the reproductivity that is of the essence of gender is surely a radical denial of reality.

The Caitlyn Jenner affair, one reporter recently observed, sent Americans on a "crash course in transgender acceptance" and sent Europe even further, "toward an even higher plane . . . a post-gender world that critics say is leaving no room for women to be women and men to be men." Recalling the checkered experiences of the postmodernist world, we may be wary of an even more venturesome, and hazardous, post-gender world. Instead of the resplendent image of Caitlyn Jenner on the cover of *Vanity Fair*, we may see the agony of people who regret the ordeal of the transformation – such operations are taking place at an ever younger age, even early childhood – and who then want to return, psychologically if not physically, to their original sex.

We might wish to take comfort today in the thought that after the initial enthusiasm for transgenderism has subsided, a more wary approach to the real problems of sexual dysfunction may prevail. Some of us had similar expectations in the case of postmodernism. When postmodernism began to lose its novelty around the turn of the century, it looked as if the humanities might revert to type – poetry retrieved from the literary critic, history rewritten as narrative, philosophy rediscovered in the classics. But that reprieve was short-lived. If postmodernism is no longer the modish term it once was, it is because its spirit has been so integrated into the culture that it no longer needs affirming or controverting. One can only hope that it won't require a new abyss, a new de Man, to transcend transgenderism.

2015

ORIGINAL PUBLICATION
CREDITS

The essays in this volume were first published as follows:

1. "Political Thinking: Ancients vs. Moderns," *Commentary*, July 1951 (here slightly abridged).

2. "The Once-Born and the Twice-Born," *Weekly Standard*, September 29, 2012.

3. "From Robespierre to ISIS: Edmund Burke's War on Terror – and Ours," *Weekly Standard*, September 29, 2014.

4. "Dissent and Dogma" (review of Matthew Arnold, *Culture and Anarchy*), *New Republic*, June 13, 1994.

5. "Meet Mr. Bagehot," *Weekly Standard*, September 9, 2013.

6. "Winston vs. the Webbs: A Preview of Obamacare," *Weekly Standard*, April 21, 2014.

7. "The Jewish Question: Then and Now," *Weekly Standard*, June 20, 2016.

8. "The Paradox of Thomas Carlyle," *Weekly Standard*, February 24, 1997.

9, "Disraeli: *Der Alte Jude*," *Weekly Standard*, May 16, 2016.

10. "What It Means to Be Educated" (review of John Henry Newman, *The Idea of a University*), *Wall Street Journal*, September 16, 1996.

11. "Evolution and Ethics, Revisited," *New Atlantis*, Spring 2014.

12. "Einstein in Theory: The Scientist as Public Intellectual," *Weekly Standard*, May 11, 2015.

13. "Lionel Trilling: Underrated," *Standpoint*, April 2009.

14. "American Democracy and Its European Critics," *Twentieth Century*, April 1952.

15. "Democratic Remedies for Democratic Disorders," *Public Interest*, Spring 1998.

16. "Compassionate Conservatism: Properly Understood," *Weekly Standard*, January 14, 2013.

17. "Our Dignified Constitution: Fourth of July Reflections on the Queen's Jubilee," *Weekly Standard*, July 16, 2012.

18. "Victorian Values, Jewish Values," *Commentary*, February 1989.

19. "For the Love of Country," *Commentary*, May 1997.

20. "Into the Abyss: From the Halls of Academia to the Cover of *Vanity Fair*," *Weekly Standard*, July 20, 2015.

INDEX

Index

A NOTE ON THE TYPE

PAST AND PRESENT *has been set in Monotype Bulmer. Based on types cut by William Martin in 1790, Bulmer builds on the structure of Caslon but anticipates the stronger geometry and dramatic contrast of stroke found in the types cut by Bodoni and the Didots. Like Baskerville and Bell, its close contemporaries, Bulmer looks best on a smooth sheet, a fact that no doubt contributed to the popularity of American Type Founders' 1928 revival of the face. ‡‡ Bulmer is notable for its upright carriage and its strong color on the page. The italic is equally strong in color, yet provides a decorative quality that makes a fine counterpoint to the formality of the roman.*

DESIGN & COMPOSITION BY CARL W. SCARBROUGH